SONGS OF PRAISE

*A Psalter Devotional
for Orthodox Women*

SYLVIA LEONTARITIS

ANCIENT FAITH PUBLISHING
CHESTERTON, INDIANA

Songs of Praise: A Psalter Devotional for Orthodox Women
Psalter text (translation) © 2016 Ancient Faith Publishing
Additional material © 2018 Sylvia Leontaritis

All rights reserved. No part of this publication may be reproduced by any means, electronic, mechanical, photocopying, recording, scanning, or otherwise, without the prior written permission of the Publisher.

Published by:
  Ancient Faith Publishing
  A Division of Ancient Faith Ministries
  P.O. Box 748
  Chesterton, IN 46304

ISBN: 978-1-944967-52-9

Printed in the United States of America

25 24 23 22 21   18 17 16 15 14 13 12 11 10 9 8 7 6 5 4 3

CONTENTS

Introduction 5

What Is a Psalter Group? 8

The Saints on Reading the Psalter 10

Prayers before Reading the Psalter 15

KATHISMA 1   17
The Pen Is Mighty   25

KATHISMA 2   32
The Struggle Is Real   41

KATHISMA 3   48
Sisterhood in Christ   60

KATHISMA 4   66
Crowned with Silver   77

KATHISMA 5   84
Beauty in the Broken   95

KATHISMA 6   102
Letters to the Theotokos   115

KATHISMA 7   122
The Orthodox Home   134

KATHISMA 8   142
Refuge   151

KATHISMA 9   158
Seek Him in the Wilderness   169

KATHISMA 10   176
The So-Called Perfect Life   188

KATHISMA 11   194
My Nest   208

KATHISMA 12   214
Fireflies   225

KATHISMA 13   232
The Pharisee in Me   242

KATHISMA 14   248
My Beautiful Mess   258

KATHISMA 15   266
A Homemaker's Prayer   277

KATHISMA 16   284
The World Needs More Love (Letters)   293

KATHISMA 17   300
Unsocial Media   312

KATHISMA 18   320
Raising Arrows   330

KATHISMA 19   338
Through the Intercessions   349

KATHISMA 20   356
Do ~~Good~~ Better   364

Topical Index to the Psalter as a Book of Needs   382

INTRODUCTION

*Forever, O Lord, Your word is firmly fixed in the heavens;
Your truth endures to all generations.*
PSALM 118:89

ear Friend,

I'm so glad you're holding this book in your hands. It was a pretty intimidating task, writing pages that will go between the God-inspired words of the Holy King and Prophet David. The verse "Let the words of my mouth and the meditation of my heart / Be acceptable in your sight, / O Lord, my strength and my Redeemer" (Ps. 19:14 NKJV) was constantly on my lips as I worked to write about topics relevant to Orthodox women today.

We have so many treasures in the Orthodox Faith. Our traditions run deep into the Old Testament, including the praying of the Psalms. The Psalter is considered the prayer book of the Church and is used in every service. Christ Himself recited the Psalms, even while He was on the Cross. St. Arsenios of Cappadocia used the Psalms as a Book of Needs; we have included a brief index to the needs he identified with each psalm as an appendix so that you may use them for your own spiritual benefit. St. Basil the Great tells us, "A psalm is a city of refuge from the demons, a means of inducing help from the angels, a weapon in fears by night, a rest from toils by day, a safeguard for infants, an adornment for those at the height of their vigor, a consolation for the elders, a most fitting ornament for women."[1]

Fourteen years ago, I was invited by a dear presbytera to join the Psalter group she was organizing. At that time, I had no idea what a

---

1 *The Psalter According to the Seventy,* Holy Transfiguration Monastery, 1997, p. 22.

Psalter group was and didn't even own a Psalter, but she assured me I'd love it. She was right. (See the following section for an explanation of what a Psalter group is and how to find one or form one in your own community.)

Since then, while I'm still a part of her groups, I also organize groups on my blog, *Adventures of an Orthodox Mom*. These groups have become a foundation for the community that has grown out of my tiny nook of the internet and a force that spiritually and physically connects Orthodox women (and men) worldwide. I anticipate the start of each forty-day fasting period so that our groups can commence and I can once again read the poetic verses of St. David together with my beloved sisters in Christ. The only thing I don't love about our groups is that they end.

My hope is that this book will inspire women everywhere to make the art of praying the Psalter part of their daily routine. I pray it will encourage each of us to put down our devices, let go of the trivial and temporary connections they entice us with, and reach for something better that will connect us eternally.

Make the following pages feel like home to you—highlight, scribble, circle, dog-ear, tape photos, and refer back to them whenever your heart needs a hug.

- » When you're anxious or afraid, open this book.
- » When your heart is heavy, open this book.
- » When you feel completely alone and don't think anyone understands, open this book.
- » When you feel like throwing in the towel, open this book.
- » When you feel like scrolling through social media, open this book.
- » When everything is going absolutely perfectly, open this book.

Pour yourself a cup of coffee or tea and allow the sweet honey of the psalms to ooze into the broken crevices of your heart and make it whole again.

I'm so grateful to be walking hand in hand with you as we strive to learn God's ways and offer up these songs of praise.

Your sister in Christ,

Sylvia

One practical note: The Psalter text in this volume is the same as that found in *The Ancient Faith Psalter.* However, while that Psalter presents the kathismata in the order in which they are prescribed for daily reading in the Church, we have placed them in the standard numerical order to avoid confusion. We have also numbered the psalms according to the Septuagint rather than the Hebrew text. (This translation does not include Psalm 151.) The original Psalter does not include verse numbers. They have been added here for ease of reference, but they may not exactly match those in other versions of the Psalter.

WHAT IS A PSALTER GROUP?

Psalter groups have been around for many years. Generations before us prayed the psalms the same way we are doing today, some of them even having memorized the entire book. It is an age-old tradition—one that I am forever grateful to have been introduced to.

When I joined my first Psalter group more than fourteen years ago, I had no idea they would become such an important part of my spiritual journey. Each time a forty-day fast (Advent or Great Lent) approaches, my heart anticipates the beginning of our groups. I look forward to having that precious Psalter book tucked in my bag alongside me, to open and be strengthened by it whenever an opportunity presents itself. It's a quiet time that I look forward to each day. And by *quiet*, I don't mean the things around me are quiet—those things rarely are—but rather, a hush comes over my soul whenever I open my Psalter and read.

Reading the psalms together with brothers and sisters from all around the world is a beautiful gift. I love knowing that I'm reading such powerful words alongside other struggling Orthodox Christians. Praying the psalms together creates a special bond, a spiritual connection to those people whose names we remember each day along with our readings.

How It Works

The Psalter is divided into twenty sections, or kathismata. So to start a group, all you need is twenty people willing to commit to reading one kathisma per day. Each kathisma takes approximately fifteen to twenty minutes to read.

On the first day of the fast, each person begins reading a different kathisma. For example:

- » On Day One, Maria would begin on Kathisma 1, I would read Kathisma 2, you would read Kathisma 3, and so on.
- » On Day Two, Maria would read Kathisma 2, I would read Kathisma 3, and you would read Kathisma 4.

We continue in this manner until we reach the end—Kathisma 20. And with twenty people each reading one kathisma per day, between them the Psalter is being read in its entirety every day of that fasting period. On the twenty-first day, we begin again where we started, individually reading the entire Psalter a total of twice during the forty days.

I know it sounds confusing, but I promise once you get started, you'll see it's much simpler than it sounds. Finding a Psalter group is easy. You can either join one of the groups I organize on my blog or, as many others have done, start a group in your own parish or community.

If you're up to the task and stick with it, it will become more a part of you with each reading. As the saints in the beginning of this book told us, reading the psalms is of much benefit to our souls. But no effort toward Christ is without its temptations. If you miss a reading, don't despair—simply jump back in and keep going. You'll get better each time, and the psalms will find their natural place in the rhythm of your daily life. Don't let the fear of not being able to keep up—or any other fear—stop you from embarking on this worthwhile journey.

This book includes the entire Psalter, broken up into individual kathismata. We have set the Psalter text with wide margins for note-taking. Each kathisma is followed by a devotional reflection and about four blank pages for journaling. (Some extra journaling pages fall at the end of the book.) So this book is ideal for use either in a Psalter group or for reading and journaling through the Psalter on your own. Blessed journey!

THE SAINTS ON READING THE PSALTER

St. Basil the Great

No other book so glorifies God as does the Psalter. It profits the soul; it glorifies God together with the angels, and exalts and extols with a powerful voice, and imitates the angels. At times, it flogs the demons and drives them out, and causes them much weeping and injury. It prays to God for kings and princes, and for the whole world. With the Psalter you can pray to God even for yourself, for it is the greatest and most exalted of books.

This book called the Psalter is like a great sea: for as the water of the sea is never diminished or exhausted by the outpouring of its rivers and streams, neither does the chanting of the Psalter ever fail. The Psalter has been called bravery and boldness before God for the salvation of the soul, for there is great reward in fasting, and in bows, and in the reading of the Psalter.

If, brother, you say that you are weak, and cannot perform this rule, being but flesh—look up into the air, and see how the sun and the moon and the stars do not rest day or night from following their path, performing the commandments of the Lord, and how this fiery creation does not eat, or drink, or look for the torment to come, but, rather, fears God, and performs His command without ceasing. You, brother, though flesh, have clothing for your body. If you are in want, you eat and drink, and sleep as is needed. There are those who get up at midnight, and worship, and pray to God, and occupy themselves with handiwork, and yet give thanks to their Maker for all things. And again he says, How weak and infirm is the nature of water, and yet it fears the Lord. Day and night it continues to ebb and flow, washing not only men, but also their darkness, giving drink to cattle, and birds, and beasts, and creeping things, and pouring itself out upon the earth. And you, brother, how is it that you neither examine nor attend to yourself? With God, all things are possible, but with man, nothing is possible. Simply take courage and be strong, and God will help you.

For David says, 'Wait thou on the Lord, and keep His way, and He shall promote thee, that thou shalt possess the land' [Ps. 36:34]; so let not a single day pass without singing from the Psalter. If for some reason, you are obliged to set it aside, mark the place, and begin again the next morning, not stopping out of slothfulness. For, as Peter, the chief of the apostles, says, 'One day of our life is with the Lord as a thousand years, and a thousand years as one day', and it makes no difference. For all the seasons of this world, brethren, turn like a wheel. Today there is sun, and, tomorrow, darkness, and rain and snow. Today, there are parties and weddings, and tomorrow, weeping and despondency. But if you take action to save your soul, you will correct your speech and learn the commandments of God, and He will open your eyes, so that you might understand the wonders of the Law of the Lord.

The great John Chrysostom was asked by the brethren, 'Is it good to lay aside the Psalter?' He replied, 'It would be better for the sun to fall from its orbit, than to neglect reading the Psalter, for it is of great benefit to study the psalms, and to read the Psalter diligently. For all spiritual books are profitable for us, and grieve the demons, but there is none like the Psalter.' Let us, then, take heed.[2]

A psalm implies serenity of soul; it is the author of peace, which calms bewildering and seething thoughts. For, it softens the wrath of the soul,

---

2 D. M. James, trans., *A Psalter for Prayer* (Jordanville, NY: Holy Trinity Publications, 2011), pp. 78–80.

and what is unbridled it chastens. A psalm forms friendships, unites those separated, conciliates those at enmity. Who, indeed, can still consider an enemy him with whom he has uttered the same prayer to God? So that psalmody, bringing about choral singing, a bond, as it were, toward unity, and joining the people into harmonious union of one choir, produces also the greatest of blessings, charity. A psalm is a city of refuge from the demons, a means of inducing help from the angels, a weapon in fears by night, a rest from toils by day, a safeguard for infants, an adornment for those at the height of their vigor, a consolation for the elders, a most fitting ornament for women. It peoples the solitudes; it rids the market place of excesses; it is the elementary exposition of beginners, the improvement of those advancing, the solid support of the perfect, the voice of the Church. It brightens the feast days; it creates a sorrow which is in accordance with God. For, a psalm is the work of angels, a heavenly institution, the spiritual incense.[3]

St. Augustine

The singing of psalms adorns the soul, summons angels to one's aid, drives away demons, dispels darkness, and produces holiness. It strengthens the mind of a sinful man; it atones for sin; it is like holy alms. It increases faith, hope, and love; it shines like the sun, it cleanses like water, it cauterizes like fire, and it soothes like oil. It puts the Devil to shame and reveals God; it extinguishes the lusts of the flesh, and is the oil of mercy, the lot of the joyful, and the chosen portion of angels. It banishes contentiousness, calms all anger, and curtails wrath; it is unceasing praise of God.

The singing of psalms is like honey. It is the preferred hymn before God; it wards off every sin, predisposes to love; it transcends all, fulfills all, teaches all, and reveals all. It exalts the soul, cleanses the lips, gladdens the heart, erects a tall pillar, enlightens a man, and calms the

---

3 *The Psalter According to the Seventy*, p. 22.

senses. It destroys every evil, and points to the way of perfection. Whosoever has the memory and love of it, has also the fear and praise of God in his heart, and will never fall away therefrom, nor will his petition be lost, but he will rejoice before God at the last.

It is silence of the mind, and harbinger of peace. For the psalms pray for the future, sigh for the present, repent of the past, rejoice in good works, and call to mind the joy of the heavenly Kingdom. Often a session of psalm-singing produces a shield of righteousness, and shines the light of truth against the demonic powers. It is the comfort of elders, an adornment for the young, and the maturity and perfection of the intellect. It teaches always to pray more attentively to Christ God, the helper and benefactor, who by the lips of the Prophet ordained these psalms.[4]

St. John Maximovich

Perhaps, it will happen that you will die without having once in your life read in full the Psalter of David. . . . You will die, and only then will good people read over your lifeless body this holy Psalter, which you had no time even to open while you lived on earth! Only then, at your burial, will they sing over you the wondrously instructive, sweetly wise but alas, to you completely unknown words of David: 'Blessed are the undefiled in the way, who walk in the law of the Lord. . . . Blessed are they who search His testimonies, who keep His revelations, and seek Him with their whole heart.' Do you hear? Blessed are they who search His testimonies, seek out the revelations of the Lord; and you had no time to even think of them! What will your poor soul feel then, your soul to which every word of the psalmist, repeated by a reader or chanter over your coffin, will sound as a strict reproach that you never read this sacred book? Open it now, before it is too late, this wondrous book of the Prophet King. Open it and read with attention at the very least the 118th Psalm and you will involuntarily feel that your heart becomes

---

4 *A Psalter for Prayer,* pp. 81–82.

humble, soft, that in the words of David are the words of the merit of God, and you will repeat involuntarily, many times with a sighing heart, the verse of this Psalm: I have gone astray like a sheep that is lost; seek out Thy slave, O Lord![5]

St. John Chrysostom

If we keep vigil in church, David comes first, last, and central. If early in the morning we want songs and hymns, first, last, and central is David again. If we are occupied with the funeral solemnities of those who have fallen asleep, or if virgins sit at home and spin, David is first, last, and central. O amazing wonder! Many who have made little progress in literature know the Psalter by heart. Nor is it only in cities and churches that David is famous; in the village market, in the desert, and in uninhabitable land, he excites the praise of God. In monasteries, among those holy choirs of angelic armies, David is first, last, and central. In the convents of virgins, where are the communities of those who imitate Mary; in the deserts where there are men crucified to the world, who live their life in heaven with God, David is first, last, and central. All other men at night are overcome by sleep. David alone is active, and gathering the servants of God into seraphic bands, he turns earth into heaven, and converts men into angels.[6]

---

5 St. John Maximovich, *Shanghai Diocesan Bulletin 503* (Nov. 24, 1941).
6 *The Psalter According to the Seventy*, p. 21.

PRAYERS
BEFORE READING THE PSALTER

In the name of the Father and of the Son and of the Holy Spirit. Amen.

O Heavenly King, Comforter, Spirit of Truth, everywhere present and filling all things, Treasury of blessings and Giver of life, come and abide in us, cleanse us from every stain, and save our souls, O Good One.

Holy God, Holy Mighty, Holy Immortal One, have mercy on us. *(3x)*

Glory to the Father and to the Son and to the Holy Spirit, both now and forever and to the ages of ages. Amen.

O Most Holy Trinity, have mercy on us. O Lord, cleanse us from our sins. O Master, pardon our iniquities. O Holy One, visit and heal our infirmities for Your name's sake.

Lord, have mercy. *(3x)*

Glory to the Father and to the Son and to the Holy Spirit, both now and forever and to the ages of ages. Amen.

Our Father in heaven, hallowed be Your name. Your kingdom come; Your will be done on earth as it is in heaven. Give us this day our daily bread. And forgive us our trespasses as we forgive those who trespass against us. And lead us not into temptation, but deliver us from the evil one.

Most Holy Trinity, God and Creator of the whole world, come and direct my heart to begin with understanding and to end with good works this divinely inspired book of the Holy Spirit uttered through the lips of David, which I now desire to recite, unworthy though I am. Knowing well my own ignorance, I fall down before You and pray, begging Your help, O Lord: direct my mind and make my heart steadfast, that I may not grow weary because of the words my lips read, but that I may be gladdened with the understanding of what I read and may be prepared for the doing of the good works that I learn. Enlightened by good deeds, may I become a citizen of the land that is at Your right hand with all Your elect. And now, O Master, bless me, that, having sighed from my heart, I may sing with my heart, I may sing with my tongue, saying:

O Come, let us worship and fall down before Christ. O Come, let us worship and bow down before Christ, our King. O Come, let us worship and fall down before Christ, our King and our God.

Through the prayers of our holy Fathers, Lord Jesus Christ our God, have mercy on us and save us. Amen.

At the end of each kathisma recite the following:

Glory to the Father, and to the Son, and to the Holy Spirit, both now and ever and unto the ages of ages. Amen.

Alleluia, Alleluia, Alleluia. Glory to You, O God. (*twice*)

Alleluia, Alleluia, Alleluia, Glory to You. O God our hope, O Lord, glory to You. Lord have mercy on (*name of each person in your group*).

KATHISMA 1

PSALM 1

1. Blessed is the man who walks not in the counsel of the wicked, nor stands on the path of sinners, nor sits in the seat of scoffers;
2. but his delight is in the law of the Lord, and on His law he meditates day and night.
3. He is like a tree planted by streams of water, that yields its fruit in its season, and its leaf does not wither.
   In all that he does, he prospers.
4. The wicked are not so, but are like chaff which the wind drives away.
5. Therefore the wicked will not stand in the judgment, nor sinners in the congregation of the righteous;
6. for the Lord knows the way of the righteous, but the way of the wicked will perish.

PSALM 2

1. Why do the nations conspire, and the peoples plot in vain?
2. The kings of the earth set themselves, and the rulers of the people have assembled, against the Lord and His Anointed, saying,
3. "Let us burst their bonds asunder and cast their cords from us."

4 He who sits in the heavens laughs; the Lord has them in derision.
5 Then He will speak to them in His wrath and terrify them in His fury.
6 But I have been made King by Him on Zion, His holy hill, telling the decree of the Lord:
7 "The Lord said to Me, 'You are My Son, this day have I begotten You.' "
8 Ask of me, and I will give You the nations for Your inheritance, and the ends of the earth as Your dominion.
9 You shall break them with a rod of iron and dash them in pieces like a potter's vessel.
10 Now therefore, O kings, be wise; be warned, O rulers of the earth.
11 Serve the Lord with fear, and rejoice in Him with trembling.
12 Accept correction, lest He be angry and you perish from the righteous way; for His wrath is quickly kindled.
Blessed are all who take refuge in Him.

PSALM 3

1 O Lord, how many are my foes! Many are rising
2 against me; many are saying of me, "There is no help for him in God."
3 But You, O Lord, are a shield about me, my glory and the lifter of my head.
4 I cry aloud to the Lord, and He answers me from His holy hill.

5 I lie down and sleep; I wake again, for the Lord sustains me.
6 I am not afraid of ten thousands of people who have set themselves against me round about.
7 Arise, O Lord! Deliver me, O my God!
For You strike all my enemies on the cheek; You break the teeth of the wicked.
8 Deliverance belongs to the Lord; Your blessing be upon Your people!

PSALM 4

1 The Lord hears me when I call to Him!
You have given me room when I was in distress; have compassion on me and hear my prayer.
2 O sons of men, how long will you be slow of heart? How long will you love vain words and seek after lies?
3 But know that the Lord has done wonderful things for His Holy One: the Lord hears when I call to Him.
4 Be angry, but sin not; feel compunction on your beds for what you say in your hearts.
5 Offer a sacrifice of righteousness and put your trust in the Lord.
6 There are many who say, "Oh, that we might see some good!"
The light of Your countenance has left its imprint on us, O Lord!
7 You have put more joy in my heart than they have when their grain and wine abound.

In peace and confidence I will both lie down and sleep; for You alone, O Lord, cause me to dwell in hope. 8

PSALM 5

Give ear to my words, O Lord; give heed to my groaning. 1

Hearken to the sound of my cry, my King and my God, for to You do I pray. 2

O Lord, in the morning You hear my voice; in the morning I prepare a sacrifice for You and watch. 3

For You are not a God who delights in wickedness; evil may not sojourn with You. 4

The boastful may not stand before Your eyes; You hate all evildoers. 5

You destroy those who speak lies; the Lord abhors bloodthirsty and deceitful men. 6

But I, through the abundance of Your mercy, will enter Your house; I will worship toward Your holy temple in the fear of You. 7

Lead me, O Lord, in Your righteousness because of my enemies; make Your way straight before me. 8

For there is no truth in their mouth; their heart is destruction, their throat is an open sepulcher, they flatter with their tongue. 9

Make them bear their guilt, O God; let them fall by their own counsels; 10
because of their many transgressions cast them out, for they have rebelled against You.

11 But let all who take refuge in You rejoice, let them
      ever sing for joy;
     and defend them, that those who love Your name
      may exult in You.
12 For You bless the righteous, O Lord; You cover
      him with favor as with a shield.

PSALM 6

1 O Lord, rebuke me not in Your anger nor
     chasten me in Your wrath.
2 Have mercy on me, O Lord, for I am weak; heal
     me, for my bones are troubled.
3 My soul also is sorely troubled. But You, O Lord—
     how long?
4 Turn, O Lord, save my life; deliver me for the sake
     of Your mercy.
5 For in death there is no remembrance of You; in
     Sheol who can give You praise?
6 I am weary with my moaning; every night I flood
     my bed with tears; I drench my couch with my
     weeping.
7 My eye wastes away because of grief; it grows
     weak because of all my foes.
8 Depart from me, all you workers of evil; for the
     Lord has heard the sound of my weeping.
9 The Lord has heard my supplication; the Lord
     accepts my prayer.
10 All my enemies shall be ashamed and sorely
     troubled; they shall turn back and be put to
     shame in a moment.

PSALM 7

O Lord my God, I have set my hope on You; save me from all my pursuers and deliver me, 1

lest like a lion they rend me, dragging me away with none to rescue. 2

O Lord my God, if I have done this, if there is wrong in my hands, if I dealt back evil to those dealing evil to me, 3 4

then may I fall empty because of my enemy; let the enemy pursue me and overtake me, 5

and let him trample my life to the ground and lay my soul in the dust.

Arise, O Lord, in Your anger; lift Yourself up against the fury of my enemies; 6

Arise, O Lord my God, in the decree which You have commanded,

and the assembly of peoples will surround You. Over it take Your seat on high. 7

The Lord shall judge the people. Give me justice, O Lord, according to my righteousness and according to the integrity that is in me. 8

Oh, let the evil of the wicked come to an end, but establish the righteous, 9

You who sound the depths of hearts and reins, O righteous God.

My righteous help is from God, who saves the upright in heart. 10

God is a righteous judge, strong and patient, who does not make His wrath felt every day. 11

12 If you will not repent, God will whet His sword; He has bent His bow and made it ready.
13 On it He has fitted instruments of death; He has fashioned His arrows for those who rage.
14 Behold, the wicked man conceives evil, and is pregnant with mischief, and brings forth lies.
15 He makes a pit, digging it out, and falls into the hole which he has made.
16 His mischief returns upon his own head, and on his own pate his violence descends.
17 I will give to the Lord the thanks due to His righteousness, and I will sing praise to the name of the Lord, the Most High.

PSALM 8

1 O Lord, our Lord, how majestic is Your name in all the earth, for Your glory is chanted above the heavens;
2 out of the mouths of babes and infants, You have fashioned perfect praise in response to Your foes, to still the enemy and the avenger.
3 When I look at Your heavens, the work of Your fingers, the moon and the stars which You have established;
4 what is man that You are mindful of him, or the son of man that You take care of him?
5 You have made him a little lower than the angels; You have crowned him with glory and honor;

You have given him dominion over the works of 6
  Your hands; You have put all things under his 7
  feet,
all sheep and oxen, and also the beasts of the field, 8
  the birds of the air, and the fish of the sea,
  whatever passes along the paths of the sea.
O Lord, our Lord, how majestic is Your name in
  all the earth!

✥ ✥ ✥

THE PEN IS MIGHTY

Give ear to my words, O Lord; give heed to my groaning.
PSALM 5:1

The most peaceful time of day for me is the wee morning hours, when everyone else is still asleep and the house is blanketed in a quiet slumber. The soft sunlight begins to stretch itself across the room, and the birds chirp happily outside my window. I make a fresh pot of coffee and retreat to my spot at the kitchen table with my Bible. It's my favorite time to pray, study, and spend time with God.

For several years now I've been prayer journaling. I read a certain chapter from the Bible and then write out the parts that stand out most to me. Later on, I usually look up commentaries on those verses by the holy fathers. This helps me dig deep into the Scriptures and learn more about what they mean. I also write out any special prayers I have that day—prayers for things going on with my husband's work or my children, or if anyone is sick, or whatever things are pressing on my heart.

Somehow, when the ink flows from my pen and across the page, my stress and worries flow out with it. It's my way of handing all those things over to God. Everything is put into perspective for me when it's on paper. Joys feel greater, and burdens feel lighter. When I'm finished, I give thanks.

Another thing I like to do is make a list of five things I'm grateful for each day. Not the big things that I'm grateful for every day, such as our health and family, but the little things that make each day beautiful and unique.

My lists usually look something like this:

Today, (*date*), I'm grateful for:
1. the leaves that have begun to change colors
2. Anna's delicious gluten-free pumpkin muffins
3. a new book
4. no laundry to do!!
5. watching my boys laugh and play in the treehouse.

You can use any type of notebook as a prayer journal. I've used plain composition books, binders, and even sticky notes that I put into my journal later. My current favorite is a traveler's notebook because it holds several small notebooks neatly inside, making it easy to keep everything organized. Whatever kind of notebook you choose, it should be a place you enjoy spending time in each day.

Once you have a notebook, start by creating individual sections for all the things you want to pray for and journal about each day. My notebook has a section for my husband and each of my children, and then another section for loved ones. Then I have a separate notebook for quotes and homily notes and another for my running prayer requests. Whenever I read or hear something that inspires or uplifts me, I write it down. I want my thoughts always to be happy and positive. Even if I'm having a rough day—perhaps especially when I'm having a rough day—focusing my thoughts on all the good things in life always chases away the negative. It's hard to be discontented when you're counting your blessings.

Prayer journaling is a great way to remind yourself of all the ways God works in your life. It's a creative way to express your thoughts and feelings to God. After all, isn't that what the psalms were to David as he wrote them?

I love going back through old notebooks, reading the things I was praying for, and seeing how God allowed things to play out. Reading through those old pages of thoughts and quotes somehow strengthens me, which is why I chose to share some of my very favorite quotes with you in this book. It has also really helped me become better in praying for others, which has always been important to me despite the fact that I'm sometimes inconsistent in doing it.

My journals hold the contents of my heart—the memories I don't want to forget, questions to ask my spiritual father, prayers for those I know and those I don't. Journaling is a tangible way for me to connect with God and keep my spiritual life alive. Spilling my heart through the ink of my pen is my favorite way to savor all the beauty in the world. It reminds me that His mercies truly are new every day (Lam. 3:23).

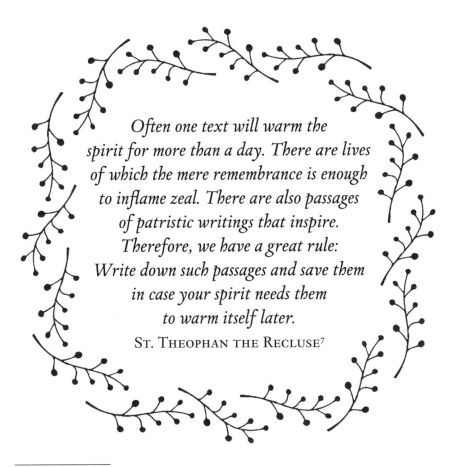

Often one text will warm the spirit for more than a day. There are lives of which the mere remembrance is enough to inflame zeal. There are also passages of patristic writings that inspire. Therefore, we have a great rule: Write down such passages and save them in case your spirit needs them to warm itself later.
ST. THEOPHAN THE RECLUSE[7]

---

7 St. Theophan the Recluse, *The Path to Salvation*, trans. Seraphim Rose (Platina, CA: St. Herman of Alaska Press, 1996), p. 248.

JOURNALING PAGES

KATHISMA 2

PSALM 9

I will give thanks to You, O Lord, with my whole heart; I will proclaim all Your wonders. 1

I will be glad and exult in You; I will sing praise to Your name, O Most High. 2

When my enemies are turned back, they will stumble and perish before Your Face. 3

For You have maintained my just cause; You have sat on the throne giving righteous judgment. 4

You have rebuked the nations, and the ungodly one has perished; You have blotted out their name forever and ever. 5

The swords of the enemy have utterly failed; their cities You have destroyed; the very memory of them has perished in tumult. 6

But the Lord reigns forever; He has established His throne for judgment, 7

and He judges the world with righteousness; He judges the peoples with equity. 8

The Lord is a stronghold for the oppressed, a stronghold in times of trouble. 9

And those who know Your name put their trust in You, for You, O Lord, have not forsaken those who attentively seek You. 10

Sing praises to the Lord, who dwells in Zion! Tell among the peoples His deeds! 11

12 For He who avenges blood is mindful of them; He
    does not forget the cry of the afflicted.
13 Have mercy on me, O Lord! Look on the affliction
    I suffer from those who hate me.
14 You lift me up from the gates of death, that I may
    recount all Your praises,
    that in the gates of the daughter of Zion I may
    rejoice in Your deliverance.
15 The nations have sunk in the pit which they made;
    in the net which they hid has their own foot
    been caught.
16 The Lord has made Himself known; He has
    executed judgment; the wicked are snared in
    the work of their own hands.
17 Let sinners be driven to Sheol, all the nations that
    forget God.
18 For the needy shall not always be forgotten, and
    the hope of the poor shall not perish forever.
19 Arise, O Lord! Let not man prevail; let the nations
    be judged before You!
20 Appoint a lawgiver over them; let the nations
    know that they are but men!
21 Why do You stand far off, O Lord? Why do You
    overlook us in times of trouble?
22 In arrogance the ungodly hotly pursue the poor;
    let them be caught in the schemes which they
    have devised.
23 For the sinner boasts of the desires of his heart,
    and the unjust one blesses himself.
24 The sinner has provoked the Lord; in his pride he
    does not seek Him; God is not before him.

25 His ways are profane at all times; Your judgments are removed from him; as for all his foes, he gains mastery over them.
26 For he says in his heart, "I shall not be moved; throughout all generations I shall not meet adversity."
27 His mouth is filled with cursing and deceit and oppression; under his tongue are mischief and iniquity.
28 He sits in ambush with the rich in order to murder the innocent.
29 His eyes stealthily watch for the poor; he lurks in secret like a lion in his covert;
30 he lurks that he may seize the poor; he seizes the poor when he draws him into his net.
 Yet he himself will fall when he has overcome the poor.
31 For he has said in his heart, "God has forgotten; He has hidden His Face; He will never see it."
32 Arise, O Lord my God, and let Your hand be lifted up; do not forget Your poor forever.
33 Why does the wicked renounce God and say in his heart, "You will not call to account!"
34 But You do see, for You perceive suffering and pain, that You may take them into Your hands;
 the poor man commits himself to You; You have been the helper of the fatherless.
35 Break the arm of the sinner and evildoer; may his sin be sought for and not be found.
36 The Lord is king forever and ever; the nations shall perish from His land.

37 O Lord, You will hear the desire of the poor; You will strengthen their heart;

38 You will incline Your ear to do justice to the fatherless and the oppressed, so that men may not boast any more upon the earth.

PSALM 10

1 In the Lord I take refuge; how can you say to me, "Flee like a bird to the mountains"?

2 For lo, the wicked bend the bow, they have prepared their arrows for the quiver, to shoot in secret at the upright in heart.

3 They have pulled down what You have built, and what has the Righteous done?

4 The Lord is in His holy temple; the Lord's throne is in heaven; His eyes behold the poor; His eyelids test the sons of men.

5 The Lord tests the righteous and the wicked; one that loves violence hates his own soul.

6 On the wicked He will rain coals of fire and brimstone; a scorching wind shall be the portion of their cup.

7 For the Lord is righteous; He loves righteous deeds; His Face looks upon honor.

PSALM 11

1 Save me, O Lord; for there is no longer any that is godly; for truth has vanished from among the sons of men.

2 Everyone utters lies to his neighbor; with flattering lips and a double heart they speak.
3 May the Lord cut off all flattering lips, the tongue that makes great boasts,
4 those who say, "With our tongue we will prevail; our lips are with us; who is our master?"
5 "Because of the suffering of the poor, because the needy groan, I will now arise," says the Lord; "I will set myself for salvation and not draw back from it!"
6 The Lord's words are pure words, like silver refined in a furnace on the ground, purified seven times.
7 You, O Lord, shall protect us and preserve us from this generation forever.
8 On every side the wicked prowl, yet according to Your greatness You have greatly exalted the sons of men.

PSALM 12

1 How long, O Lord? Will You forget me until the end? How long will You turn away Your Face from me?
2 How long shall I take counsel in my soul and have sorrows in my heart every day? How long shall my enemy be exalted over me?
3 Consider and answer me, O Lord my God; lighten my eyes, lest I sleep in death;

4 lest at any time my enemies say, "I have prevailed against him"; lest my persecutors exult if ever I am shaken.
5 But I have trusted in Your mercy; my heart shall rejoice in Your salvation.
I will sing to the Lord, because He has dealt bountifully with me, and I will sing psalms to the name of the Lord Most High.

PSALM 13

1 The fool says in his heart, "There is no God."
They are corrupt; they do abominable deeds; there is none that does good.
2 The Lord looked down from heaven and saw all the sons of men, to see if there are any that have understood, that sought after God.
3 They have all fallen away; they are all alike unprofitable; there is none that does good, no, not one.
4 Shall they never learn, those who practice lawlessness, those who eat up my people as they eat bread? They do not call upon God.
5 There they were in great terror, where there was no cause for fear, for God dwells among the righteous.
6 They tried to confound the plans of the poor, but the Lord is his hope.
7 Who will bring about the salvation of Israel out of Zion?

When the Lord brings back the captives of His
people, Jacob will rejoice and Israel be glad.

PSALM 14

O Lord, who shall sojourn in Your tabernacle? 1
Who shall dwell on Your holy mountain?
He who walks blamelessly, and does what is right, 2
and speaks truth from his heart;
who has not spoken deceitfully with his tongue, 3
and does no evil to his neighbor, nor takes up a
reproach against his brother;
in whose eyes the Evil One is despised, but who 4
glorifies those who fear the Lord;
who swears an oath to his neighbor and does not
break it;
who does not put out his money at interest, and 5
does not take a bribe against the innocent.
He who does these things shall never be moved. 6

PSALM 15

Preserve me, O God, for in You do I take refuge. 1
I say to the Lord, "You are my Lord, for You have 2
no need of my goodness."
As for the saints in the land, the Lord has made 3
them wonderful; all His will is accomplished in
them.
The weaknesses of those who choose another god 4
have been multiplied: "I will not attend their

  meetings of blood or take their names upon
   my lips."
5 The Lord is the portion of my inheritance and of
   my cup; You restore to me my inheritance.
6 The lines have fallen for me in the best of places;
   yes, I have an excellent heritage.
7 I will bless the Lord who gives me counsel; even
   in the night my heart instructs me.
8 I keep the Lord always before me; because He is at
   my right hand, I shall not be shaken.
9 Therefore my heart is glad, and my soul rejoices;
   my body also dwells securely.
10 For You will not leave my soul in Sheol nor let
   Your Holy One see corruption.
11 You have shown me the paths of life; You will fill
   me with the joy of Your countenance; at Your
   right hand are pleasures forevermore.

PSALM 16

1 Hear a just cause, O Lord; attend to my cry! Give
   ear to my prayer from lips free of deceit!
2 From You let my vindication come! Let my eyes
   see the right!
3 If You try my heart, if You visit me by night, if
   You test me,
  You will find no wickedness in me; my mouth
   does not transgress.
4 With regard to the works of men, by the word of
   Your lips I have avoided the ways of the violent.

5 My steps have held fast to Your paths; my feet have not slipped.
6 I call upon You, for You will answer me, O God; incline Your ear to me, hear my words.
7 Wondrously show Your steadfast love, O Savior of those who seek refuge from their adversaries at Your right hand.
8 Keep me as the apple of the eye; hide me in the shadow of Your wings from the wicked who
9 despoil me, my deadly enemies who surround me.
10 They close their hearts to pity; with their mouths they speak arrogantly.
11 They track me down; now they surround me; they set their eyes to cast me to the ground.
12 They are like a lion eager to tear, as a young lion lurking in ambush.
13 Arise, O Lord! Confront them, overthrow them!
   Deliver my life from the wicked by Your sword, from men by Your hand, O Lord, from men whose portion in life is of the world.
14 May their belly be filled with what You have stored up for them; may their children have more than enough; may they leave something over to their babes.
15 As for me, I shall behold Your Face in righteousness; when I awake, I shall be satisfied with beholding Your form.

✠ ✠ ✠

THE STRUGGLE IS REAL

*The Lord is a stronghold for the oppressed,
a stronghold in times of trouble.*
PSALM 9:9

When I first heard the term *spiritual warfare*, I conjured up images of ascetics in the desert battling dark and evil spirits. Never did I imagine that regular people, like you and me, were engaged in that war. Yet we are.

The more I read about battling our thoughts and passions, the more I realized how many battles I was losing in my daily life. It was as if I was walking through a battlefield that my soul was too blinded by the world even to see. Suddenly, life looked like a minefield, each situation and decision I faced being potentially spiritually destructive. I had to learn how to better navigate the path of my soul by recognizing the threats and learning to protect myself against the attacks of the enemy. By not arming myself with prayer, I was going to war defenseless.

One thing I consistently found, when reading books like *Unseen Warfare* or the *Philokalia*, was the practice of the Jesus Prayer. I was no stranger to the art of the Jesus Prayer—the monastics at the monasteries we visited often whispered the prayer aloud when working, and I had been given a prayer rope when I attended church camp in middle school—but I had only the faintest idea of the true power behind the words: *Lord Jesus Christ, Son of God, have mercy on me, a sinner.*

When a monastic is tonsured, he or she is given a prayer rope as one of his or her few possessions. The prayer rope is to serve as a spiritual sword, a weapon against the devil.

As Orthodox Christians, we don't believe in assurance of salvation. Instead we've been taught how to fight for our salvation.

St. Anatoly of Optina wrote, "Are you fighting against your passions? Fight, fight, and be good soldiers of Christ! Do not give in to evil and do not be carried away by the weakness of the flesh."[1]

Christ said that the Kingdom of heaven is taken by force (Matt. 11:12). St. Paul encourages us to fight the good fight, reminding us that our battle is not against flesh and blood (Eph. 6:12). This means we cannot afford to remain idle while the devil wages war against us. We have to fight for our souls and struggle toward salvation every single day. We have the teachings not only of the Holy Scriptures but of countless saints and holy fathers who tell us everything we need to know about spiritual warfare. But are we listening? Are we taking their advice and putting it into practice, or are we reading it and then letting their words fall by the wayside?

Every morning since I've been a mother, I make sure my children are armed for battle. We do morning prayers, and then I cross their foreheads with holy oil—their armor. They each take a small piece of antidoron and a sip of holy water—their strength. Then we make sure they have their weapons—a cross and a prayer rope. Now that they're getting older and this has become a daily morning habit, even if I'm somewhere else in the house, they will go to our prayer corner, do morning prayers, and arm themselves before coming downstairs to start the day.

My oldest, who is now a teenager, no longer goes through the steps as animatedly as he once did or as his little brothers still do. However, he himself has now entered the arena. As their mother, my job is to make sure my children are equipped, through the life and teachings of the Church, for the battles they'll encounter. Though they may grow weary of my lectures, they will not tire of the incredible stories of the lives of the saints. And even if they do, I won't stop telling them.

As an Orthodox woman in the world, I need to remind myself

---

1 *Living Without Hypocrisy: Spiritual Counssels of the Holy Elders of Optina* (Jordanville, NY: Holy Trinity Publications, 2005), p. 11.

constantly to fight against the spirit of secularism and to keep my eyes on Christ instead of on the next sparkling thing that threatens to divert my attention from Him.

The struggle is real, dear sisters, but so is the prize. Press forward with the sweet words of the Jesus Prayer on your lips, and keep fighting the good fight!

*Life is spiritual warfare.
If you're not fighting,
you're losing.*
—St. Kosmas Aitolos

JOURNALING PAGES

KATHISMA 3

PSALM 17

I will love You, O Lord, my God. The Lord is my refuge, my strength and my deliverer. 1

My God is my helper; in Him will I hope: my shield and the horn of my salvation, my defender. 2

I call upon the Lord with songs of praise, and I shall be saved from my enemies. 3

The waves of death engulfed me; the torrents of perdition assailed me; 4

The pangs of Sheol surrounded me; the snares of death overtook me. 5

In my distress I called upon the Lord; to my God I cried for help. 6

From His temple He heard my voice, and my cry to Him reached His ears.

Then the earth reeled and rocked; the foundations also of the mountains were troubled and shaken, because He was angry with them. 7

Smoke went up from His anger and devouring fire from His mouth that kindled coals into flame. 8

He bowed the heavens and came down; thick darkness was under His feet. 9

He rode upon cherubim and flew, borne upon the wings of the wind. 10

11 He made darkness His hiding place; as His canopy around Him, dark thunderclouds hung in the sky.
12 Out of the brightness before Him there broke through the clouds hailstones and coals of fire.
13 Then the Lord thundered from heaven, and the Most High uttered His voice.
14 He shot His arrows and scattered them; with many lightning flashes He routed them.
15 Then the fountains of waters appeared, and the foundations of the earth were laid bare
at Your rebuke, O Lord, at the blast of the breath of Your anger.
16 He reached from on high and took me; He drew me out of the deep waters.
17 He delivered me from my strong enemies and from those who hated me, for they were mightier than I.
18 They overtook me in the day of my calamity, but the Lord was my firm support.
19 He brought me forth into a spacious place; He will deliver me, because He delights in me.
20 The Lord will reward me according to my righteousness; according to the cleanness of my hands He will repay me.
21 For I have kept the ways of the Lord and have not acted wickedly toward my God.
22 For all His judgments are before me, and His statutes have not departed from me.
23 I shall be blameless toward Him, and I will keep myself from iniquity.

24 The Lord will reward me according to my righteousness, according to the cleanness of my hands in His sight.
25 With the holy You will be holy; with the innocent You will be innocent.
26 With the great You will be great, and with the perverse You will be perverse.
27 For You will save a humble people, and you will humble the eyes of the proud.
28 For You will light my lamp, O Lord my God; You will enlighten my darkness.
29 For with Your help, I shall be delivered from a troop, and in my God I shall leap over the wall.
30 As for my God, His way is perfect; the words of the Lord are tried by fire; He is the defender of all who hope in Him.
31 For who is God but the Lord? And who is God but our God?
32 It is God who girded me with strength and made my way blameless.
33 He made my feet like hinds' feet and set me secure on the heights.
34 He trained my hands for war so that my arms can bend a bow of bronze.
35 You have given me the shield of salvation, and Your right hand has supported me.
Your instruction set me on the straight path forever; Your instruction itself taught me.
36 You gave length to my steps under me, and unwavering was my stride.
37 I will pursue my enemies and catch them, and I will not turn back till they are destroyed.

38 I will crush them, and they will not be able to stand; they will fall under my feet.
39 For You girded me with strength for war; You bound the feet of all my adversaries beneath me.
40 You made my enemies turn their backs to me, and those who hated me You have utterly destroyed.
41 They cried out, but there was none to save; they cried to the Lord, but He did not answer them.
42 I will beat them fine as dust before the wind; I cast them out like the mire of the streets.
43 You deliver me from strife with the peoples; You make me the head of the nations.
44 A people whom I had not known became my servants; as soon as they heard me, they obeyed me.
45 But my sons became strangers to me; they lied to me; my sons, having estranged themselves, grew old, and limping, they strayed from their path.
46 The Lord lives; blessed be my God! Exalted be the God of my salvation!
47 God gives vengeance to me and subdues peoples under me.
48 You who deliver me from my angry enemies will exalt me above those who rise against me; You will deliver me from the unrighteous man.
49 For this I will extol You, O Lord, among the nations and sing praise to Your name.
50 God works wonders for the salvation of His King and deals mercifully with David His Anointed and his seed forever.

PSALM 18

1. The heavens are telling the glory of God; and the firmament proclaims His handiwork.
2. Day to day pours forth speech, and night to night declares knowledge.
3. There are no tongues or words in which their voices are not heard.
4. Their proclamation has gone out into all the earth and their words to the ends of the universe.
5. He has set His tabernacle in the sun; like a bridegroom coming forth from his bridal chamber, like a strong man it runs its course with joy.
6. Its rising is from one end of the heavens and its circuit to the other end; no one can escape from its heat.
7. The law of the Lord is perfect, converting souls; the testimony of the Lord is sure, making children wise.
8. The precepts of the Lord are right, rejoicing the heart; the commandment of the Lord is bright, enlightening the eyes.
9. The fear of the Lord is pure, enduring forever and ever; the judgments of the Lord are true and righteous altogether.
10. More to be desired are they than gold or precious stones and sweeter than honey or the honeycomb.
11. So Your servant keeps them; in keeping them there is great reward.

12 Who can discern his transgressions?
Cleanse me from my hidden faults, and preserve
13   Your servant from those which are foreign to me.
If they do not have dominion over me, I shall be blameless and innocent of great transgression.
14 Then the words of my mouth will be pleasing to You;
and the meditation of my heart will be before You always, O Lord, my helper and my Redeemer.

PSALM 19

1 The Lord answer you in the day of trouble; the name of the God of Jacob protect you!
2 May He send you help from the sanctuary and give you support from Zion!
3 May He remember all your sacrifices and regard with favor your whole burnt offerings!
4 May He grant you your heart's desire and fulfill all your plans!
5 We will rejoice in your salvation and be exalted in the name of the Lord our God. May the Lord fulfill all your petitions!
6 Now I know that the Lord has saved His Anointed; He will answer him from His holy heaven; salvation is in the mighty deeds of His right hand.
7 Some trust in chariots and some in horses; but we will call upon the name of the Lord our God.

Their feet have been fettered; they have fallen, 8
    but we have risen and stand upright.
Save the king, O Lord; hear us on the day we call. 9

PSALM 20

In Your strength the king rejoices, O Lord, and 1
    greatly exults in Your salvation!
You have given him his heart's desire and have not 2
    withheld the request of his lips.
For You meet him with goodly blessings; You 3
    have placed upon his head a crown of precious
    stones.
He asked life of You, and You gave it to him— 4
    length of days forever and ever.
His glory is great in Your salvation; splendor and 5
    majesty You have bestowed upon him.
You will give him a blessing forever and will make 6
    him glad with the joy of Your presence.
For the king hopes in the Lord; and through the 7
    mercy of the Most High he shall not be shaken.
May your hand be felt by all your enemies; may 8
    your right hand find all those who hate you.
You will make them like a blazing oven on the day 9
    when you appear; the Lord will confound them
    in His wrath; and fire will consume them.
You will destroy their fruit from the earth and 10
    their seed from among the sons of men.
For they planned evil against you; they have 11
    devised plots which will not succeed.

12 For you will put them to flight; you will make them face your remnant.
13 Be exalted, O Lord, in Your strength! We will sing and praise Your power!

PSALM 21

1 O God, my God, attend to me! Why have You forsaken me?
Why are You so far from helping me, from the words of my groaning?
2 O my God, I cry by day, but You do not answer, and by night, but find no rest.
3 But You dwell in the sanctuary, the Praise of Israel.
4 In You our fathers hoped; they hoped in You, and You delivered them.
5 To You they cried and were saved; in You they hoped and were not disappointed.
6 But as for me, I am a worm and no man, a reproach of men and the outcast of the people.
7 All who see me mock me; they open their lips and wag their heads:
8 "He hoped in the Lord—let Him deliver him; let Him save him, if He was pleased in Him."
9 Yet You are He who took me from the womb; You have been my hope from my mother's breasts.
10 Upon You was I cast from my birth; from my mother's womb, You have been my God.
11 Be not far from me, for trouble is near, and there is none to help me.

12 Many bullocks encircle me; strong bulls surround me.

13 They open their mouths against me like ravenous and roaring lions.

14 I am poured out like water, and all my bones are out of joint; my heart is like wax melted within my breast.

15 My strength is dried up like a potsherd, and my tongue cleaves to my throat; You have brought me down into the dust of death.

16 For many dogs are round about me; a company of evildoers closes in upon me; they have pierced my hands and feet.

17 They count all my bones; they stare and gloat over me.

18 They divided my garments among them, and for my raiment they cast lots.

19 But You, O Lord, do not remove Your help from me! Hasten to my aid!

20 Deliver me from the sword, my afflicted soul from the power of the dog!

21 Save me from the mouth of the lion, my lowliness from the horns of the wild bulls.

22 I will declare Your name to my brethren; in the midst of the assembly I will confess You.

23 Praise Him, all who fear the Lord! All you sons of Jacob, glorify Him, and stand in awe of Him, all you offspring of Israel!

24 For He has not despised or abhorred the supplication of the poor man, nor has He turned His Face from me, but He has heard me when I cried to Him.

25 From You is my praise; in the great congregation
I will praise You; I will pay my vows in the
presence of those who fear You.
26 The poor shall eat and be satisfied; those who seek
the Lord shall praise Him; their hearts shall live
forever.
27 All the ends of the earth shall remember and turn
to the Lord; all the families of the nations shall
bow down before Him.
28 For the Kingdom belongs to the Lord, and He
Himself rules over the nations.
29 All the mighty ones of the earth have bowed
down; before Him shall bow all who go down
into the earth.
30 Yes, my soul lives for Him, and my children will
serve Him.
31 The coming generation shall be told of the Lord,
and they will declare His righteousness to a
people yet unborn whom the Lord has made.

PSALM 22

1 The Lord is my shepherd; I shall not want; He
2 makes me lie down in green pastures;
3 He establishes me beside the waters of rest; He
restores my soul.
He leads me in the paths of righteousness for His
name's sake.
4 Even though I walk through the valley of the
shadow of death, I will fear no evil; for You are
with me;

Your rod and Your staff, they comfort me.
You prepare a table before me in the presence of my enemies; 5
You anoint my head with oil: oh, how exquisite is the inebriation of Your cup!
Your mercy, O Lord, shall follow me all the days of my life, and I shall dwell in the house of the Lord forever. 6

PSALM 23

The earth is the Lord's and its fullness, the world and all that dwell in it. 1
He has founded it upon the seas and established it upon the rivers. 2
Who shall ascend the mountain of the Lord, and who shall stand in His holy place? 3
He that is innocent in his hands and pure in his heart, who has not lifted up his soul to vanity nor sworn deceitfully to his neighbor. 4
He will receive a blessing from the Lord and mercy from God his Savior. 5
This is the generation of those who seek Him, who seek the Face of the God of Jacob. 6
Lift up your gates, O you princes, and be lifted up, O everlasting doors, and the King of glory shall enter. 7
Who is this King of glory? The Lord, strong and mighty, the Lord, mighty in battle. 8

9 Lift up your gates, O you princes, and be lifted up, O everlasting doors, and the King of glory shall enter.
10 Who is this King of glory? The Lord of hosts, He is the King of glory!

✠ ✠ ✠

SISTERHOOD IN CHRIST

More to be desired are they than gold or precious stones and sweeter than honey or the honeycomb.
PSALM 18:10

It can be hard in today's ever-changing society to find like-minded women to accompany us on our journey toward Christ—women who understand the desire to be modest, prayerful, and zealous in the service of others. How refreshing to have someone who will calm our worries with responses like "Let's pray about it together," or "Forgive her, she doesn't understand," or "That dress is beautiful but not really appropriate for a woman of Christ." I know I cherish the people in my life who offer me godly advice (and practice it in their own daily lives) instead of adding fuel to a fire or encouraging me to be of the world.

But a question I hear often is, Where do I find those women? Where can we find women who will motivate and inspire us in godly ways instead of the ways of the world?

Chances are they're closer than you think. There are probably a few in your church community already. You don't have to know them well to extend an invitation to coffee or a play date at the park. Chances are they're looking for the same kind of godly sisterhood.

If you're not sure where to begin, talk to your priest about getting a women's group started. Or why not invite several women to your home to pray an akathist and have brunch? At the beginning of the school year last year, I invited a couple of Orthodox mothers over to my house to pray the *Akathist to the Mother of God, Nurturer of Children*. We all wrote down the names of our children and godchildren and took turns reading the service. Afterward, we had cake and coffee. It was such a beautiful experience, and I hope to continue doing it.

If you're part of a smaller community and feel there's no one at all to connect with, maybe you should join an email or online group. If you're not keen on the internet, you might start a text group with mothers you know from other places. Whatever you do, keep searching and pray about it. Don't give up. God will provide exactly who you need.

In the meantime, we can always work on bettering ourselves as godly sisters in Christ. Recognize the areas you're weak in and be persistent in becoming stronger. Ask for God's help through the prayers of the Theotokos.

Below are a few qualities I believe a true sister in Christ should possess. She should:

» stand her ground in the Faith and constantly pursue holiness, not worldliness;
» be loyal and honest in all things;
» be modest in dress, speech, and behavior;
» refrain from gossip;
» offer correction with love;
» love unconditionally and accept you as you are;
» get up when she falls and learn from each stumble;
» accept constructive criticism.

Which of these qualities do you already possess? Which areas do you need to work on?

True friendship is like a rare Indian plant: however hard I tried to describe it, I would be unable to convey a proper understanding of it to someone who had no experience of it.
—Saint John Chrysostom

JOURNALING PAGES

KATHISMA 4

PSALM 24

1 To You, O Lord, I lift up my soul. O my God, in You I trust;
2 let me not be put to shame; let not my enemies exult over me.
3 Yes, let none that wait for You be put to shame; let them be ashamed who are wantonly treacherous.
4 Make me to know Your ways, O Lord; teach me Your paths.
5 Lead me in Your truth and teach me, for You are the God of my salvation; for You I wait all the day long.
6 Be mindful of Your mercy, O Lord, and of Your steadfast love, for they have been from of old.
7 Remember not the sins of my youth or my transgressions;
according to Your steadfast love, remember me for Your goodness' sake, O Lord!
8 Good and upright is the Lord; therefore He instructs sinners in the way.
9 He leads the humble in what is right and teaches the humble His way.
10 All the paths of the Lord are steadfast love and faithfulness for those who keep His covenant and His testimonies.

11 For Your name's sake, O Lord, pardon my guilt, for it is great.
12 Who is the man that fears the Lord? Him will He instruct in the way that he should choose.
13 His soul shall dwell with the blessed and his children shall possess the land.
14 The friendship of the Lord is for those who fear Him, and He makes known to them His covenant.
15 My eyes are ever toward the Lord, for He will pluck my feet out of the net.
16 Turn to me and be gracious to me, for I am lonely and afflicted.
17 Relieve the troubles of my heart and bring me out of my distresses.
18 Consider my affliction and my trouble and forgive all my sins.
19 Consider how many are my foes and with what violent hatred they hate me.
20 Oh, guard my life and deliver me; let me not be put to shame, for I take refuge in You.
21 May integrity and uprightness preserve me, for I wait for You.
22 Redeem Israel, O God, out of all his troubles!

PSALM 25

1 Judge me, O Lord, for I have walked in my innocence; I have hoped in the Lord and shall not be moved.

Prove me, O Lord, and try me; test with fire my reins and my heart.

For Your mercy is before my eyes, and I rejoice in Your truth.

I have not sat with a vain council, nor do I consort with transgressors;

I have hated the company of evildoers, and I will not sit with the ungodly.

I will wash my hands in innocence, and go about Your altar, O Lord,

proclaiming Your name, telling of all Your wonders.

O Lord, I love the beauty of Your house and the place where Your glory dwells.

Do not destroy my soul with the ungodly nor my life with bloodthirsty men,

in whose hands are evil devices and whose right hands are full of bribes.

But as for me, I have walked in my innocence; redeem me and have mercy on me.

My foot has stood firm on the righteous path; I will bless You, O Lord, in the congregation.

PSALM 26

The Lord is my light and my salvation; whom shall I fear?

The Lord is the defender of my life; of whom shall I be afraid?

When evildoers assailed me to eat up my flesh, my adversaries and foes, they stumbled and fell.

3   Though an army encamp against me, my heart shall not fear; though war rise up against me, yet I am confident in this.
4   One thing have I asked of the Lord—that will I seek after—
that I may dwell in the house of the Lord all the days of my life, to behold the beauty of the Lord and to look upon His temple.
5   For He hid me in His shelter in the day of my afflictions;
He concealed me in the cover of His tabernacle; He set me high upon a rock.
6   And now, behold, my head has been lifted up above my enemies;
I will go round and offer in His tabernacle the sacrifice of joy; I will sing psalms and make melody to the Lord.
7   Hear my voice, O Lord, when I cry aloud; have mercy on me and answer me!
8   My heart said to You, "I have earnestly sought Your Face; Your Face, O Lord, will I seek."
9   Turn not Your Face away from me; do not turn away from your servant in anger.
Be my helper, forsake me not, and do not overlook me, O God my Savior!
10   For my father and my mother have forsaken me, but the Lord has taken me to Himself.
11   Instruct me in Your way, O Lord, and lead me on a right path because of my enemies.
12   Give me not up to the will of my oppressors; for false witnesses have risen against me, and wicked men have lied to themselves.

I believe that I shall see the goodness of the Lord   13
    in the land of the living.
Wait on the Lord; be courageous and let your   14
    heart be strengthened; yes, wait on the Lord.

PSALM 27

To You, O Lord, will I call; O my God, be not   1
    silent to me.
May You never be silent to me, lest I become like
    those who go down to the pit.
Hear the voice of my supplication as I pray to You,   2
    as I lift up my hands toward Your holy temple.
Take me not away with sinners, and do not   3
    destroy me with those who are workers of
    iniquity,
who speak peace with their neighbors while evils
    are in their hearts.
Requite them according to their work, and   4
    according to the evil of their deeds;
requite them according to the work of their hands;
    render them their due reward.
Because they do not regard Your works, O Lord,   5
    nor the work of Your hands,
You will break them down and build them up no
    more.
Blessed be the Lord! For He has heard the voice of   6
    my supplication.
The Lord is my helper and my defender; in Him   7
    my heart hopes, and so I am helped.

My flesh has revived, and I willingly give praise to Him.
8 The Lord is the strength of His people and the saving defender of His Anointed.
9 O Lord, save Your people and bless Your inheritance: be their shepherd and lift them up forever!

PSALM 28

1 Offer to the Lord, O you sons of God, offer young rams to the Lord! Ascribe to the Lord glory and honor.
2 Offer to the Lord the glory due His name; worship the Lord in His holy court.
3 The voice of the Lord is upon the waters; the God of glory thunders; the Lord, upon many waters!
4 The voice of the Lord is powerful; the voice of the Lord is full of majesty.
5 The voice of the Lord breaks the cedars; the Lord will break the cedars of Lebanon.
6 He will tear them in pieces, even the calf of Lebanon; the beloved one is like a young wild bull.
7 The voice of the Lord divides the flames of fire;
8 the voice of the Lord shakes the wilderness; the Lord will shake the wilderness of Kadesh.
9 The voice of the Lord strengthens the hinds and will strip the forest bare; in His temple everyone speaks of His glory.

The Lord sits enthroned over the flood; the Lord will sit enthroned as King forever. 10

The Lord will give strength to His people; the Lord will bless His people with peace! 11

PSALM 29

I will extol You, O Lord, for You have drawn me up and have not caused my foes to rejoice over me. 1

O Lord my God, I cried to You, and You healed me. 2

O Lord, You have brought up my soul from Sheol, restored me to life from among those gone down to the pit. 3

Sing to the Lord, O you His saints, and give thanks for the remembrance of His holiness. 4

For there is destruction in His anger, but life in His will. 5
Weeping shall tarry for the night, but joy shall be in the morning.

As for me, I said in my prosperity, "I shall never be moved." 6

O Lord, in Your good pleasure you added strength to my beauty; but You hid Your Face, and I was dismayed. 7

To You, O Lord, I cry; to my God I make supplication: 8

"What profit is there in my blood when I go down to destruction? 9

      Will the dust praise You? Or will it declare Your truth?"
10   The Lord heard and had compassion on me; the Lord has become my helper.
11   You have turned for me my mourning into joy; You have torn off my sackcloth and girded me with gladness,
12   that my glory may sing praise to You and that I may not be pierced with sorrow.
      O Lord my God, I will give thanks to You forever!

PSALM 30

1   In You, O Lord, do I hope; let me never be put to shame; deliver me in Your righteousness and rescue me!
2   Incline Your ear to me; rescue me speedily! Be a protecting God for me, a house of refuge to save me!
3   You are my strength and my refuge; for Your name's sake You will guide me and keep me.
4   You will take me out of the net which is hidden for me, for You, O Lord, are my defender.
5   Into Your hands I commit my spirit; You have redeemed me, O Lord, God of truth.
6   You have hated those who idly persist in vanities; but I have hoped in the Lord.
7   I will rejoice and be glad in Your mercy, because You have seen my affliction;

You have saved my soul from adversities and have not delivered me into the hand of the enemy; You have set my feet in a broad place. 8

Have mercy on me, O Lord, for I am afflicted; my eye is wasted from indignation, my soul and my body also. 9

For my life is spent with sorrow and my years with sighing. 10

My strength fails because of my poverty, and my bones waste away.

I have become a reproach among all my adversaries, a horror to my neighbors, an object of dread to my acquaintances; 11

those who saw me in the street fled from me.

I have passed out of mind like one who is dead; I have become like a broken vessel. 12

For I heard the slander of many that live on every side: they gathered together against me as they plotted to take away my life. 13

But I hoped in You, O Lord: I said, "You are my God. My lots are in Your hand." 14

Deliver me from the hand of my enemies and persecutors. 15

Let Your Face shine on Your servant; save me in Your mercy! 16

Let me not be put to shame, O Lord, for I call on You; let the ungodly be put to shame and brought down to Sheol. 17

Let the lying lips be dumb which speak insolently against the righteous in pride and contempt. 18

How abundant is the multitude of Your goodness, which You have laid up for those who fear You 19

    and wrought for those who hope in You, in the
        presence of the sons of men!
20 In the secret place of Your presence You will hide
        them from the plots of men;
    You will hold them safe in Your tabernacle from
        the strife of tongues.
21 Blessed be the Lord, for He has worked wonders
        of mercy for me in a fortified city.
22 But I said in my alarm, "I am driven far from the
        sight of Your eyes."
    Therefore You heard the voice of my supplications
        when I cried to You.
23 Love the Lord, all you His saints, for the Lord
        seeks for truth and abundantly requites those
        who act haughtily.
24 Take courage and let your heart be strengthened,
        all who hope in the Lord!

PSALM 31

1 Blessed is he whose transgression is forgiven,
        whose sin is covered.
2 Blessed is the man to whom the Lord imputes no
        iniquity and in whose mouth there is no deceit.
3 When I declared not my sin, my body wasted
        away through my groaning all day long.
4 For day and night Your hand was heavy upon
        me; my strength was dried up as by the heat of
        summer.
5 I acknowledged my sin to You, and I did not hide
        my iniquity.

I said, "I will confess my transgressions to the
   Lord"; then You forgave the ungodliness of my
   heart.
For his sin, everyone who is godly will offer   6
   prayer to You at a fitting time; and the rush of
   great waters shall not reach him.
You are my hiding place from the affliction that   7
   surrounds me; my joy, to deliver me from those
   who encompass me.
"I will instruct you and teach you the way you   8
   should go; I will set my eyes upon you."
Be not like a horse or a mule, without   9
   understanding, which must be curbed with bit
   and bridle, or else it will not keep with you.
Many are the pangs of the wicked; but mercy   10
   surrounds him who trusts in the Lord.
Be glad in the Lord and rejoice, O righteous, and   11
   shout for joy, all you upright in heart!

✠ ✠ ✠

CROWNED WITH SILVER

You have hated those who idly persist in vanities;
but I have hoped in the Lord.
PSALM 30:6

The other day at the park, I saw a little old couple walking along the edge of the duck pond. They strolled hand in hand, pausing momentarily to toss bread crumbs into the water.

Now you should know that I think elderly people are the sweetest thing ever and have been known to secretly snap photographs of them. They charm me. The lines of their faces are like lines of a book, each telling a different part of the story. A story I long to know.

As a little girl, I'd watch my great-grandmother brushing her long silver locks in the morning. She'd brush her hair, pull it over her shoulder to braid, then twist and pin it into a bun at the nape of her neck. It's the only way she ever wore her hair.

Where are the elderly women today? Those silver-haired women in modest dresses have been replaced by ladies with perfectly coifed hair wearing designer labels.

Women today are bombarded with promises of everlasting youth. They're terrified of growing old and vow to fight it with all they've got. To say I don't understand the fear of aging would be a lie. Of course, I get it. It could be scary watching yourself transform into a different person, maybe a less beautiful person by worldly standards, but it could also be an incredibly beautiful thing. I've always been an old soul, and so part of me feels as if my physical appearance is catching up to my heart. The world needs more women who are courageous enough to do what makes them holy—not happy. Women should be confident in their natural beauty. Our appearance should reflect modesty and virtue rather than a secular spirit. You don't have to be twenty to be beautiful. True beauty moves in stages, and we should trust God to continue transforming us into what He created us to be.

Titus 2:3–5 tells us older women should be "reverent in behavior, not slanderers, not given to much wine, teachers of good things—that they admonish the young women to love their husbands, to love their children, to be discreet, chaste, homemakers, good, obedient to their own husbands, that the word of God may not be blasphemed."

I pray to live long enough to be that little old lady sitting in a rocking chair with knitting needles in her lap and a worn-out Bible in her hands, offering morsels of the wisdom acquired through a lifetime of struggle and learning from her many mistakes.

Over the past few years, my husband and I have been finding strands of silver in our hair, and it's such an amazing thing—to be growing old with the one you love. Aging is a sign of life, and life is a blessing.

Beside my bed, I have icons of some of my favorite Orthodox women—the Theotokos; Ss. Nonna, Emmelia, and Anthousa—mothers of the Holy Hierarchs; St. Sophia and her daughters; St. Julitta and her son Kyrikos; St. Sevastiane and St. Kalliope—patrons saints of my mother, grandmother, great-grandmother, and myself. Countless times, I've stood before them and implored their intercessions. *They* are the women I look up to, the ones I want to be like "when I grow up." And I'll tell you, I can't imagine a single one of them fretting over gray hairs or crow's feet.

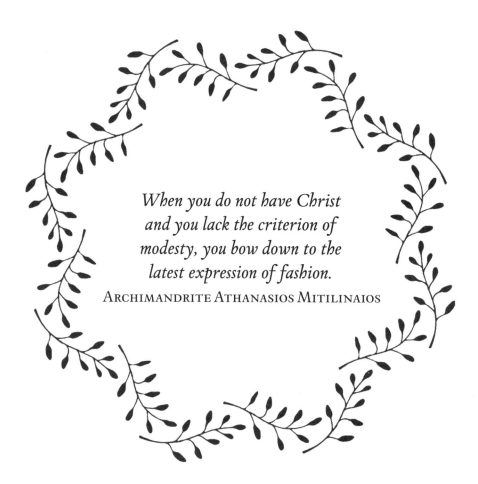

When you do not have Christ and you lack the criterion of modesty, you bow down to the latest expression of fashion.
ARCHIMANDRITE ATHANASIOS MITILINAIOS

JOURNALING PAGES

KATHISMA 5

PSALM 32

R ejoice in the Lord, O you righteous! Praise befits the just. 1

Praise the Lord with the lyre; make a melody to Him with the harp of ten strings! 2

Sing to Him a new song; sing praises beautifully with a loud shout. 3

For the word of the Lord is right, and all His works are faithfulness. 4

He loves mercy and judgment; the earth is full of the mercy of the Lord. 5

By the Word of the Lord the heavens were made, and all their host by the Spirit of His mouth. 6

He gathers the waters of the sea as in a bottle; He put the deeps in storehouses. 7

Let all the earth fear the Lord; let all the inhabitants of the world be moved because of Him! 8

For He spoke and they were made; He commanded and they were created. 9

The Lord frustrates the counsel of the nations; He brings to naught the plans of the people and the reasoning of princes. 10

But the counsel of the Lord stands forever, the thoughts of His heart from generation to generation. 11

12 Blessed is the nation whose God is the Lord,
    the people whom He has chosen for His own inheritance!
13 The Lord looked down from heaven and saw all the sons of men;
14 He looks from His prepared habitation on all the inhabitants of the earth:
15 He who alone fashions their hearts and observes all their deeds.
16 A king is not saved by his great army; a giant is not delivered by his great strength.
17 The war horse is a vain hope for victory; despite its great might, it cannot save.
18 Behold, the eyes of the Lord are on those who fear Him, on those who hope in His mercy,
19 that He may deliver their soul from death, and keep them alive in famine.
20 Our soul waits for the Lord; He is our helper and defender.
21 Our heart shall rejoice in Him, and we have hoped in His holy name.
22 Let Your mercy, O Lord, be upon us, as we have set our hope on You.

PSALM 33

1 I will bless the Lord at all times; His praise shall continually be in my mouth.
2 My soul makes its boast in the Lord; let the meek hear and be glad.

O magnify the Lord with me, and let us exalt His name together!	3
I sought the Lord with diligence, and He heard me and delivered me from all my tribulations.	4
Draw near to Him and be illumined, so your faces shall not be ashamed.	5
This poor man cried and the Lord heard him, and saved him out of all his troubles.	6
The angel of the Lord will encamp around those who fear Him and will deliver them.	7
O taste and see that the Lord is good! Blessed is the man who hopes in Him!	8
O fear the Lord, all you His saints, for those who fear Him have no want!	9
The rich have become poor and hungry; but those who seek the Lord with diligence shall lack no good thing.	10
Come, O sons, listen to me; I will teach you the fear of the Lord.	11
What man is there who desires life, loving to see good days?	12
Keep your tongue from evil and your lips from speaking deceit.	13
Depart from evil and do good; seek peace and pursue it.	14
The eyes of the Lord are upon the righteous, and His ears are open to their supplication.	15
But the face of the Lord is against evildoers to cut off the remembrance of them from the earth.	16
The righteous called, and the Lord heard them and delivered them out of all their afflictions.	17

18 The Lord is near to the brokenhearted and saves the lowly in spirit.
19 Many are the afflictions of the righteous, but the Lord delivers them out of them all.
20 He keeps all his bones; not one of them shall be broken.
21 The death of sinners is wretched, and those who hate righteousness will stumble.
22 The Lord will redeem the souls of His servants; none of those who hope in Him will stumble.

PSALM 34

1 Judge, O Lord, those who wrong me; fight against those who fight against me.
2 Take hold of shield and buckler and rise for my help.
3 Draw the sword and stop the way against those who persecute me.
Say to my soul, "I am your salvation."
4 Let those be put to shame and confounded who seek after my soul.
Let those who desire evil for me be turned back and brought to dishonor.
5 Let them be as dust before the wind, with the angel of the Lord afflicting them.
6 Let their way be dark and slippery, with the angel of the Lord pursuing them.
7 For without cause they hid their snare for me; without cause they have reproached my soul.

Let a snare come upon them unawares! Let the net 8
  which they hid take them, and let them fall into
  the same snare.
Then my soul shall rejoice in the Lord, exulting in 9
  His salvation.
All my bones shall say, "O Lord, who is like You, 10
  delivering the poor out of the hand of those
  who are stronger than he, the poor and the
  needy from those who despoil him?"
False witnesses rose up and asked me of things 11
  I knew not.
They rewarded me evil for good; my soul is 12
  forlorn.
But I, when they troubled me, put on sackcloth 13
  and humbled my soul with fasting; I prayed
  with my head bowed down.
I behaved agreeably toward them as though to our 14
  neighbor or brother.
I humbled myself as one sad of countenance and
  in mourning.
But they rejoiced at my expense; they gathered 15
  together against me.
Many whips came down on me, and I knew not
  why.
They tempted me; they mocked me with 16
  contempt, gnashing at me with their teeth.
They were scattered, but they did not repent.
O Lord, when will You look on me? Deliver my 17
  soul from their mischief, my life from the lions!
Then I will confess You in the great congregation; 18
  in the mighty throng I will praise You.

19 Let not those rejoice over me who are my enemies without a cause,
   those who hate me without reason and wink to one another with the eye.
20 For they spoke peace to me; but in their fury, they conceived words of deceit.
21 They opened wide their mouths against me;
   they said, "Aha, aha, our eyes have seen his downfall."
22 You have seen, O Lord; be not silent! O Lord, be not far from me!
23 Awake, O Lord, and attend to my judgment, to my cause, my God and my Lord.
24 Judge me, O Lord, according to Your righteousness, and let them rejoice no longer at my expense.
25 Let them not say in their hearts anymore, "Aha, we have our heart's desire!"
   Let them not say anymore, "We have swallowed him up."
26 Let them be put to shame and confusion altogether who rejoice at my calamity.
   Let them be clothed with shame and dishonor who magnify themselves against me.
27 Let those who rejoice in my righteousness shout for joy and be glad and say evermore,
   "Great is the Lord, who delights in the peace of His servant!"
28 Then my tongue shall tell of Your righteousness and of Your praise all the day long.

PSALM 35

1 The transgressor has resolved to sin; there is no fear of God before his eyes.
2 For he deals craftily with himself, so that he may not find out his iniquity and hate it.
3 The words of his mouth are mischief and deceit; he is not inclined to act wisely and do good.
4 He plots mischief while on his bed; he sets himself in a way that is not good; he spurns not evil.
5 Your mercy, O Lord, extends to the heavens, Your truth to the clouds.
6 Your righteousness is like the mountains of God; Your judgments are like the great deep; O Lord, You will save men and beasts.
7 How You have multiplied Your mercy, O God! The sons of men take refuge in the shadow of Your wings.
8 They feast on the abundance of Your house, and You give them drink from the river of Your delights.
9 For with You is the fountain of life; in Your light we shall see light.
10 Continue Your mercy on those who know You, and Your righteousness to the upright of heart!
11 Let not the foot of the arrogant come upon me, nor the hand of the wicked drive me away.
12 There the evildoers lie prostrate; they are cast out, unable to rise.

PSALM 36

1 Be not jealous of the wicked nor envious of evildoers.
2 For they will soon fade like the grass and wither like the green herb.
3 Hope in the Lord and do good; so you will dwell in the land and be fed with its wealth.
4 Take delight in the Lord, and He will give you the desires of your heart.
5 Disclose your struggles to the Lord; hope in Him, and He will act.
6 He will cause your righteousness to shine forth as the light and your judgment as the noonday.
7 Be still before the Lord and submit yourself to Him;
be not jealous of him who prospers in his way, of the man who transgresses the law.
8 Refrain from anger, and forsake wrath. Let not envy lead you to evil deeds.
9 For the wicked shall be cut off; but those who wait for the Lord shall possess the land.
10 Yet a little while, and the wicked will be no more; though you look well at his place, he will not be there.
11 But the meek shall inherit the earth and delight themselves in the fullness of peace.
12 The sinner will plot against the righteous and gnash his teeth at him;

13 but the Lord shall laugh at him, for He sees that his day is coming.
14 The wicked have drawn their swords and bent their bows to bring down the poor and needy, to slay the upright in heart.
15 Let their sword enter their own heart and their bows be broken.
16 Better is the little the righteous has than the great wealth of sinners.
17 For the arms of the wicked shall be broken, but the Lord upholds the righteous.
18 The Lord knows the days of the blameless, and their heritage will abide forever.
19 They are not put to shame in evil times; in the days of famine they have abundance.
20 But the wicked perish; the enemies of the Lord, at the moment of being honored and exalted, like smoke they vanish away.
21 The wicked borrows and will not pay back, but the righteous has compassion and gives;
22 for those who bless the Lord shall possess the land, but those who curse Him shall be cut off.
23 The Lord guides the steps of man, and He will delight in his ways.
24 Though he fall, he shall not be cast headlong, for the Lord is the stay of his hand.
25 I have been young and now am old, yet I have not seen the righteous forsaken or his children begging bread.
26 He is merciful and ever lending, and his children shall be blessed.

27 Depart from evil and do good; so shall you abide
     forever.
28 For the Lord loves justice; He will not forsake His
     saints; they shall be preserved forever.
29 The sinners will be chastised, and the children of
     the ungodly shall be destroyed;
   but the righteous shall inherit the earth and dwell
     upon it forever.
30 The mouth of the righteous will meditate on
     wisdom, and his tongue will speak justice.
31 The law of his God is in his heart, and his steps
     will not slip.
32 The wicked watches the righteous and seeks to
     slay him.
33 The Lord will not abandon him into his hands or
     let him be condemned when he is brought to
     trial.
34 Wait for the Lord and keep to His way, and He
     will exalt you to possess the land;
   you will look on the destruction of the wicked.
35 I have seen a wicked man overbearing and
     towering like a cedar of Lebanon.
36 Again I passed by, and lo, he was no more; though
     I sought him, he could not be found.
37 Maintain innocence and behold uprightness, for
     there is posterity for the man of peace.
38 But transgressors shall be altogether destroyed;
     the posterity of the ungodly shall be cut off.
39 The salvation of the righteous is from the Lord;
   He is their defender in the time of tribulation;

the Lord shall help them and deliver them; He   40
shall deliver them from the wicked and save
them, because they have hoped in Him.

✠ ✠ ✠

BEAUTY IN THE BROKEN

*The Lord is near to the brokenhearted
and saves the lowly in spirit.*
Psalm 33:18

At what point in life do we start counting our struggles as joy? When do those days marked on your calendar with a broken heart become less painful, making room for sentiment instead of hurt?

The world tells us the blessed people are the ones whose lives appear perfect, the ones who have it all together. But in the Orthodox Church, we understand things quite differently. We don't believe God punishes us through our suffering, but rather that He perfects us in it.

As Orthodox Christians, we don't look to fictional characters in books or movies as role models; we look to the saints. In their lives we see how even the people closest to God suffered. In order for God to refine us, we must be put through the furnace. Rocks are turned into diamonds only by extreme pressure.

Archimandrite Vassileios, in his book *Hymn of Entry*, wrote, "Fortunate is the man who is broken in pieces and given to his brother. . . . When his time of trial comes, he will not be afraid. He will have nothing to fear."[1]

How can a person be broken in pieces and given to his brother? By gathering the pieces of himself and giving them to those around him. Each time we are hurt, each struggle that threatens to break us, is a unique piece of a story to tell, a morsel of knowledge to be passed on. We tell others of the things we know, the lessons we've learned the hard way. Sometimes those stories fall on deaf ears, and we get frustrated;

---

[1] Arch. Vassileios, *Hymn of Entry* (Crestwood, NY: SVS Press, 2011).

we regret exposing that raw, vulnerable piece of ourselves to someone who doesn't have the same depth of understanding. But then later, often much later, we realize a seed was sown after all, and we witness the miracle of it sprouting and growing into something beautiful in that person's life.

It hurts to be broken, but how we react to that pain is what determines whether it turns us into diamonds or destroys us. Pain can make us bitter and afraid, or it can make us strong and courageous so that we have nothing to fear when the hour of trial arrives yet again.

If we're patient and view suffering from just the right angle, instead of merely seeing jagged fragments of something forever ruined, we'll see a ray of light shine on those pieces, causing them to change color and shimmer in a way they never did before. There's beauty in the broken. Brokenness is what earns us the crowns of gray on our heads and the lines on our faces. It's a part of life that deserves to be embraced, even welcomed.

Some may see the pieces on the floor and find them useless and offensive. They'll cover them up to hide their imperfection, pretending nothing happened. But others, the wise ones, will see the beauty in the fragility of those shattered pieces and will bravely and gently pick them up and carry them to Christ, who will change them into something new. Again and again and again.

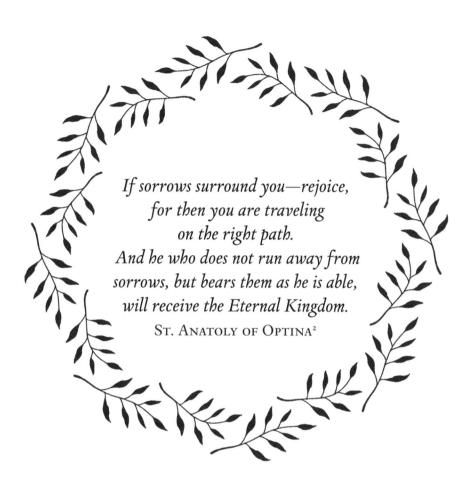

*If sorrows surround you—rejoice,
for then you are traveling
on the right path.
And he who does not run away from
sorrows, but bears them as he is able,
will receive the Eternal Kingdom.*
ST. ANATOLY OF OPTINA[2]

---

[2] *Living Without Hypocrisy*, p. 162.

JOURNALING PAGES

KATHISMA 6

PSALM 37

O Lord, rebuke me not in Your anger, nor chasten me in Your wrath. 1

For Your arrows have sunk into me, and Your hand has come down on me. 2

There is no soundness in my flesh because of Your indignation; there is no health in my bones because of my sins. 3

For my iniquities have gone over my head; they weigh like a burden too heavy for me. 4

My wounds grow foul and fester because of my foolishness; I am utterly bowed down and prostrate; all the day I go about mourning. 5 6

For my soul is filled with burning, and there is no soundness in my flesh. 7

I am utterly spent and crushed; I groan because of the tumult of my heart. 8

O Lord, all my longing is known to You; my sighing is not hidden from You. 9

My heart throbs, my strength fails me, and the light of my eyes—it also has gone from me. 10

My friends and companions stand aloof from my plague, and my kinsmen stand afar off. 11

Those who seek my life lay their snares; those who seek my hurt speak of ruin and meditate treachery all the day long. 12

13 But I am like a deaf man; I do not hear, like a dumb man who does not open his mouth.
14 I am like a man who does not hear and in whose mouth are no rebukes.
15 But in You, O Lord, have I hoped; You, O Lord my God, will answer.
16 For I pray, "Only let them not rejoice over me," who boast against me when my foot slips.
17 For I am ready to fall, and my pain is ever with
18 me. I confess my iniquity; I am sorry for my sin.
19 But those who are my foes without cause are mighty, and many are those who hate me wrongfully.
20 Those who render me evil for good are my adversaries, because I follow after good.
21 Do not forsake me, O Lord! O my God, be not far
22 from me! Make haste to help me, O Lord, my salvation!

PSALM 38

1 I said, "I will take heed to my ways, that I may not sin with my tongue";
I set a guard on my mouth so long as the sinner stood in my presence.
2 I was dumb and humbled myself and kept silence even from good words, but my grief was renewed.
3 My heart became hot within me; a fire kindled in my meditation; then I spoke with my tongue:

4 Lord, let me know my end and what is the measure of my days, that I may know what I lack.

5 Behold, you have made my days a few handbreadths, and my lifetime is as nothing in Your sight.

No, every man living is altogether vanity! Surely man goes about as a shadow!

6 Surely for naught are they in turmoil; man heaps up treasures and knows not for whom he gathers them.

7 And now, for what do I wait? Is it not the Lord? Even my existence is from you.

8 Deliver me from all my transgressions; You have made me the scorn of the fool.

9 I was dumb; I did not open my mouth, for this was from You.

10 Remove Your stroke from me; I am spent by the blows of Your hand.

11 In chastening man for his sin, You instruct him.

You make his life to be consumed like a spider's web; yes, every man is in turmoil for nothing.

12 Hear my prayer, O Lord, and give ear to my cry; hold not Your peace at my tears!

For I am Your passing guest, a sojourner, like all my fathers.

13 Spare me, that I may find the place of refreshment before I depart and am no more!

PSALM 39

1 I waited eagerly for the Lord, and He inclined to me and heard my cry.
2 He brought me up out of a pit of misery and from miry clay and ordered my way aright.
3 He put a new song in my mouth, a song of praise to our God.
Many will see and fear and put their trust in the Lord.
4 Blessed is the man whose hope is in the name of the Lord, who has not turned to vanities, to that which deceives and leads astray!
5 You have multiplied, O Lord my God, Your wondrous deeds, and in Your thoughts none can compare with You!
I proclaimed and told of them; they were more than can be numbered.
6 Sacrifice and offering You do not desire, but You have prepared a body for me;
7 burnt offering and sin offering, You have not required; so then I said, "Lo, I come."
8 In the roll of the book it is written of me: I delight to do Your will, O my God; Your law is within my heart.
9 I have proclaimed Your righteousness in the great congregation;
lo, I will not restrain my lips, as You know, O Lord.

I have not hidden Your truth within my heart; I have spoken of Your salvation. 10

I have not concealed Your mercy and Your truth from the great congregation.

O Lord, do not withhold Your mercy from me; Your mercy and Your truth have ever preserved me. 11

For evils have encompassed me without number; my iniquities have overtaken me till I cannot see; 12

they are more than the hairs of my head; my heart fails me.

Be pleased, O Lord, to deliver me; O Lord, make haste to help me! 13

Let those be put to shame and confusion who seek my life! 14

Let those who desire evil for me be turned back and brought to dishonor.

Let those who say, "Aha, aha!" be put to confusion. 15

Let all who seek You rejoice and be glad in You! 16
  Let those who love Your salvation say evermore, "God is great!"

But I am poor and needy; hasten to me, O God! 17
  You are my help and deliverer; O Lord, do not delay.

PSALM 40

Blessed is He who considers the poor and needy! The Lord will deliver Him in the day of trouble. 1

2 The Lord will protect him and keep him alive, and bless him on the earth, and not deliver him into the hands of his enemy.
3 The Lord will sustain him on his sickbed; from his illness and all his infirmities, You will heal him.
4 I said, "Lord, have mercy on me; heal my soul, for I have sinned against You."
5 My enemies say of me in malice, "When will he die and his name perish?"
6 And if one came to see me, he uttered empty words;

his heart gathered iniquity; when he goes out, he tells it abroad.
7 All my enemies whispered together about me; they devised evil against me. They uttered lawless words against me.
8 But He who fell asleep, will he not rise again?
9 For even the man to whom I had given my peace, in whom I trusted—

he who ate of my bread has lifted his heel against me.
10 But O Lord, have compassion on me and raise me up, and I shall requite them!
11 By this I know that You have delighted in me, because my enemy shall not rejoice over me.
12 But You have upheld me because of my innocence and set me before Your Face forever.
13 Blessed be the Lord, the God of Israel, from everlasting to everlasting! Amen and Amen.

PSALM 41

1. As a hart longs for flowing streams, so longs my soul for You, O God.
2. My soul thirsts for God, for the living God. When shall I come and behold the Face of God?
3. My tears have been my food day and night, while men say to me continually, "Where is your God?"
4. These things I remembered as I poured out my soul:
Yes, I will go to the place of Your wonderful tabernacle, even to the house of God,
with glad shouts and songs of thanksgiving of a multitude keeping festival.
5. Why are you cast down, O my soul, and why are you disquieted within me?
Hope in God; for I will give thanks to Him, the salvation of my countenance and my God.
6. My soul is cast down within me; therefore, I have remembered You from the land of Jordan and of Hermon, from the small mountain.
7. Deep calls to deep at the thunder of Your cataracts; all Your waves and your billows have gone over me.
8. By day the Lord will command His mercy; by night I will sing a psalm to Him—a prayer to the God of my life.
9. I will say to God, "You are my Helper; why have You forgotten me?"

Why do I go mourning because of the oppression of the enemy?
10 While my bones were breaking, my adversaries taunted me, while they said to me daily, "Where is your God?"
11 Why are you cast down, O my soul, and why are you disquieted within me?
Hope in God, for I will give thanks to Him, the help of my countenance and my God.

PSALM 42

1 Judge me, O God, and defend my cause against an ungodly people; from the deceitful and unjust man deliver me!
2 For You, O God, are my strength; why have You cast me off?
Why do I go mourning because of the oppression of the enemy?
3 O Lord, send out Your light and Your truth; let them lead me; let them bring me to Your holy mountain and to Your tabernacle!
4 And I will go to the altar of God, to God the joy of my youth;
I will give thanks to You with the lyre, O God, my God.
5 Why are you cast down, O my soul, and why are you disquieted within me?
Hope in God; for I shall again praise Him, my help and my God.

PSALM 43

We have heard with our ears, O God, and our fathers have told us what deeds You performed in their days, in the days of old: 1

With Your own hand You drove out the nations, but You planted our fathers; 2
You afflicted the peoples and cast them out.

For not by their own sword did they win the land; nor did their own arm save them, 3
but Your right hand and Your arm and the light of Your countenance; for You delighted in them.

You are my King and my God who commands deliverance for Jacob. 4

Through You we push down our foes; through Your name we tread down our assailants. 5

For not in my bow do I trust, nor will my sword save me. 6

For You have saved us from those who oppose us and have put to shame those who hate us. 7

In God will we make our boast all the day, and we will give thanks to Your name forever. 8

But now You have cast us off; You have covered us with shame; You do not go out any longer with our armies. 9

You have made us flee before our foes; and those who hated us have gotten spoil. 10

You have made us like sheep for slaughter, and have scattered us among the nations. 11

12 You have sold Your people for no price, and there was no profit in their exchange.
13 You have made us the taunt of our neighbors, the derision and scorn of those about us.
14 You have made us a byword among the nations, a laughingstock among the peoples.
15 All day long my disgrace is before me, and shame has covered my face
16 at the voice of the slanderer and reviler, because of the enemy and the avenger.
17 All this has come upon us, though we have not forgotten You or betrayed Your covenant.
18 And our heart has not turned back, but You have turned our steps aside from Your way,
19 for You have laid us low in a place of affliction, and the shadow of death has covered us.
20 If we had forgotten the name of our God or spread forth our hands to a strange god,
21 would not God have discovered this? For He knows the secrets of the heart.
22 No, for Your sake we are slain all the day long and accounted as sheep for the slaughter.
23 Awake! Why do You sleep, O Lord? Arise, and do not cast us off forever!
24 Why do You hide Your Face? Why do You forget our poverty and affliction?
25 For our soul has been bowed down to the dust; our body cleaves to the ground.
26 Arise, O Lord, and help us! Deliver us for Your name's sake!

PSALM 44

My heart overflows with a goodly theme; I address my verses to the king; my tongue is like the pen of a ready scribe.

You are the fairest of the sons of men; grace is poured upon Your lips; therefore God has blessed you forever.

Gird your sword upon Your thigh, O Mighty One, in Your glory and majesty.

Draw Your bow; ride forth in triumph, and reign for the sake of truth and meekness and righteousness.

May Your right hand teach You dread deeds!

Your arrows are sharp in the heart of the king's enemies; the peoples fall under You.

Your throne, O God, endures forever and ever; the scepter of righteousness is the scepter of Your Kingdom.

You love righteousness and hate iniquity; therefore, God, Your God, has anointed You with the oil of gladness above Your fellows.

Your robes are all fragrant with myrrh and aloes and cassia.

From ivory palaces, stringed instruments make You glad; daughters of kings are among Your ladies of honor; at Your right hand stands the queen in gold of Ophir.

Hear, O daughter, and see and incline your ear; forget your people and your father's house;

11 then the King will desire your beauty, for He is your Lord, and you shall worship Him.
12 And the people of Tyre come with gifts; even the rich among the people shall seek your favor.
13 The King's daughter is all glorious within; her robes are of cloth of gold.
14 Clad in many colors she is led to the King: after her, the virgins, her companions, are brought to You.
15 They are led in with joy and gladness; they enter the temple of the King.
16 Instead of your fathers, sons are born to you; you shall make them princes over all the earth.
17 I will cause your name to be celebrated in all generations; therefore the peoples shall praise you forever and ever.

PSALM 45

1 God is our refuge and strength, a help in the afflictions that have come upon us.
2 Therefore we will not fear if the earth be shaken, if the mountains are removed to the heart of
3 the sea; if their waters roar and are troubled, and if the mountains are shaken by His might.
4 There is a river whose streams make glad the city of God; the Most High has sanctified His tabernacle.
5 God is in the midst of her; she shall not be moved; God will help her with His countenance.

The nations were troubled, the kingdoms tottered;   6
    He uttered His voice, the earth shook.
The Lord of hosts is with us; the God of Jacob is   7
    our refuge.
Come, behold the works of the Lord, what   8
    wonders He has wrought on the earth.
He makes wars cease to the end of the earth; He   9
    will break the bow and shatter the spear and
    burn the shield with fire!
Be still and know that I am God. I am exalted   10
    among the nations; I am exalted in the earth!
The Lord of hosts is with us; the God of Jacob is   11
    our refuge.

LETTERS TO THE THEOTOKOS

At Your right hand stands the queen in gold of Ophir.
PSALM 44:9

One of my favorite services is the Paraklesis to the Theotokos—not only because the words are so beautiful and grace-filled, but because there has never been a time when I've prayed that service with all my heart and she hasn't come to my aid. Whenever I'm in need, I retreat to our icon corner, lit only by the soft glow of the vigil lamp, tie my head-covering under my chin, light the censer, and begin to chant Psalm 142.

Whenever someone tells me they're distressed about a particular situation, I suggest praying the Paraklesis, because I know the Panagia will not turn anyone away and truly is a speedy intercessor. Just as she whispered into the ear of her Son in Cana, she whispers now. And just as in Cana, even though He said His time had not yet come, Jesus honors the requests of His Mother.

Years ago, I was dealing with some health issues and needed someone to listen to the things going on in my head. Normally, I have a whole queue of women in my life who would fit that description, but this was something I didn't want to burden anyone else with. So I grabbed an empty journal from my shelf and began writing a letter to the Theotokos. I can't tell you how much this helped me. By the time I finished the letter, I was so at peace with the situation that even though I had no idea what the outcome would be, it felt resolved.

After that, writing letters seemed to be a road worth at least a short walk. As it turned out, that walk has evolved into a worthwhile journey.

Some of my letters are pages long and very specific; others are short and vague. Sometimes I know I need God's help but can't quite put my finger on why, so I implore the Theotokos for help.

Prayers aren't always answered the way we want them to be, but it's often those "unanswered" prayers that offer the most valuable lessons. If we look at them closely, we'll learn there is really no such thing as an unanswered prayer. There are only prayers that are answered differently than we expected.

Next time you're feeling overwhelmed or alone, take out a piece of paper and write a letter to the Theotokos. As a mother, she understands our struggles, our fears, the weaknesses of our flesh. As the Mother of God, she stands beside her Son, praying for those who ask for her prayers. In order for her to answer, we have to ask. Why not ask in a letter?

Orthodox Christians should have an icon of the Theotokos that they particularly love, and we should keep that icon with us, venerating it and pleading for her intercessions at all times.

ELDER JOSEPH THE HESYCHAST[1]

---

1 *Monastic Wisdom: The Letters of Elder Joseph the Hesychast* (Florence, AZ: St. Anthony's Greek Orthodox Monastery, 1999).

JOURNALING PAGES

KATHISMA 7

PSALM 46

Clap your hands, all peoples! Shout to God with loud songs of joy! 1

For the Lord, the Most High, is terrible, a great King over all the earth. 2

He subdues peoples under us and nations under our feet. 3

He has chosen His inheritance for us: the beauty of Jacob whom He loved. 4

God has gone up with a shout, the Lord with the sound of a trumpet! 5

Sing praises to our God, sing praises! Sing praises to our King, sing praises! 6

For God is the king of all the earth; sing praises with wisdom! 7

God reigns over the nations; God sits on the throne of His holiness. 8

The rulers of the people are assembled with the God of Abraham, 9

for God's mighty ones on earth have been greatly exalted!

PSALM 47

Great is the Lord, and greatly to be praised, in the city of our God and on His holy mountain; 1

2   He founded it for the joy of all the earth: Mount Zion, the city of the great King.
3   Within her citadels God is known when He defends her.
4   For lo, the kings assembled, they came on together.
5   They saw and they wondered; they were troubled, they were moved.
6   Trembling took hold of them there, pangs as of a woman in travail.
7   By a vehement wind You broke the ships of Tarshish.
8   As we have heard, so have we seen, in the city of the Lord of hosts, in the city of our God. God has established her forever.
9   We have thought of Your mercy, O God, in the midst of Your people.
10   As Your name, O God, so Your praise reaches to the ends of the earth.
11   Your right hand is filled with righteousness; let Mount Zion be glad!
Let the daughters of Judah rejoice because of Your judgments, O Lord!
12   Walk about Zion, go round about her, number her towers,
13   let your hearts consider well her strength, observe her citadels,
14   so that you may proclaim to the coming generations that the Lord is our God forever and ever;
He is our shepherd for all eternity.

PSALM 48

1. Hear this, all peoples! Give ear, all inhabitants of the world!
2. Both sons of low men and sons of high, rich and poor together!
3. My mouth shall speak wisdom; the meditation of my heart shall be understanding.
4. I will incline my ear to a proverb; I will solve my riddle in psalmody.
5. Why should I fear in times of trouble, when the iniquity of my persecutors surrounds me,
6. men who trust in their power and boast of the abundance of their riches?
7. Their brother was not able to redeem them; shall a man redeem them?
8. He will not give to God a ransom for Himself, nor the price of the redemption of His own soul;
9. He will labor in this age and live forever, for He will not see corruption,
10. while He shall see even the wise die; the fool and the stupid alike must perish and leave their wealth to strangers.
11. Their graves will be their homes forever, their dwelling places to all generations, though they called lands after their own names.
12. Man, when he was honored, did not understand, but ranked himself with senseless beasts and became like them.

13   Their way will be the cause of their fall, though
        afterward men will commend their sayings.
14   Like sheep they are appointed for Sheol; death
        shall be their shepherd;
15   but God will deliver my soul from the grasp of
        Sheol when He will receive me.
16   Be not afraid when one becomes rich, when the
        glory of his house increases.
17   For when he dies he will carry nothing away; his
        glory will not go down after him.
18   Though while he lives, a man receives flattery, and
        though he acknowledges You when You grant
        him prosperity,
19   he will go to the generation of his fathers; he will
        never more see the light.
20   Man, when he was honored, did not understand,
        but ranked himself with senseless beasts and
        became like them.

PSALM 49

1   The Lord, the God of gods, speaks and summons
        the earth from the rising of the sun to its
        setting.
2   Out of Zion shines forth the perfection of His
        beauty.
3   God, our God, shall come openly and shall not
        keep silence.
        A fire shall be kindled before Him; round about
        Him shall be a mighty tempest.

He shall call to the heavens above and to the earth, that He may judge His people:	4
Gather to Me, my venerable ones, who made a covenant with Me by sacrifice!	5
The heavens shall declare His righteousness, for God Himself is judge.	6
Hear, O my people, and I will speak to you, O Israel. I will testify to you: I am God, your God.	7
I will not reprove you for your sacrifices; your burnt offerings are continually before me.	8
I will accept no bull from your house nor he-goat from your folds.	9
For all the wild beasts of the forest are mine, the cattle on the hills and the oxen.	10
I know all the birds of the air, and the beauty of the field is mine.	11
If I should be hungry, I will not tell you, for the world is mine and all its fullness.	12
Will I eat the flesh of bulls or drink the blood of goats?	13
Offer to God the sacrifice of praise, and pay your vows to the Most High,	14
and call upon Me in the day of trouble; I will deliver you, and you shall glorify Me.	15
But to the sinner God has said, "Why do you recite my statutes, or take my covenant in your mouth?	16
For you have hated discipline, and have cast My words behind you.	17
If you saw a thief, you ran along with him, and you cast your lot with adulterers.	18

19 Your mouth has multiplied wickedness, and your tongue has framed deceit.
20 You sat and spoke against your brother; you slandered your mother's son.
21 These things you have done, and I have been silent; you thought wickedly that I should be one like yourself.
But I will rebuke you and lay the charge before you.
22 Mark these things, then, you who forget God, lest I rend and there be no deliverer!
23 The sacrifice of praise will glorify Me; there I will show him the salvation of God!"

PSALM 50

1 Have mercy on me, O God, according to Your steadfast love;
2 according to your abundant mercy, blot out my transgressions.
3 Wash me thoroughly from my iniquity and cleanse me from my sin.
4 For I know my transgressions, and my sin is ever before me.
5 Against You, You only, have I sinned and done that which is evil in Your sight,
so that You are justified in Your sentence and blameless in Your judgment.
6 Behold, I was brought forth in iniquity, and in sin did my mother conceive me.

Behold, You desire truth in the inward being; therefore, teach me wisdom in my secret heart. 7

Purge me with hyssop, and I shall be clean; wash me, and I shall be whiter than snow. 8

Fill me with joy and gladness; let the bones which You have broken rejoice. 9

Hide Your Face from my sins and blot out all my iniquities. 10

Create in me a clean heart, O God, and put a new and right spirit within me. 11

Cast me not away from Your presence, and take not Your Holy Spirit from me. 12

Restore to me the joy of Your salvation, and uphold me with a willing spirit. 13

Then I will teach transgressors Your ways, and sinners will return to You. 14

Deliver me from bloodguilt, O God, God of my salvation, and my tongue will sing aloud of Your deliverance. 15

O Lord, open my lips, and my mouth shall show forth Your praise. 16

For You have no delight in sacrifice; were I to give a burnt offering, You would not be pleased. 17

The sacrifice acceptable to God is a broken spirit; a broken and contrite heart, O God, You will not despise. 18

Do good to Zion in Your good pleasure; rebuild the walls of Jerusalem; 19

then will You delight in right sacrifices, in burnt offerings and whole burnt offerings; then bulls will be offered on Your altar. 20

PSALM 51

1   Why do you glory in your evil, O mighty man?
2   All the day your tongue is plotting unrighteousness; like a sharp razor, you have worked treachery.
3   You have loved evil more than good, and wickedness more than speaking righteousness.
4   You love all words of destruction, O deceitful tongue.
5   Therefore, may God break you down forever; may He snatch and tear you from your dwelling and uproot you from the land of the living.
6   The righteous shall see and fear and shall laugh at him, saying,
7   "See the man who would not make God his help, but trusted in the abundance of his riches and strengthened himself in his vanity."
8   But I am like a green olive tree in the house of God.
    I have trusted in the mercy of God forever and ever.
9   I will give thanks to You forever, because You have done it.
    I will wait upon Your name, for it is good, in the presence of the saints.

✠ ✠ ✠

PSALM 52

The fool says in his heart, "There is no God." 1
They are corrupt; they do abominable deeds;
 there is none who does good.
God looked down from heaven and saw all the 2
 sons of men, to see if there are any that have
 understood, that sought after God.
They have all fallen away; they are all alike 3
 unprofitable; there is none that does good, no,
 not one.
Shall they never learn, those who practice 4
 lawlessness, those who eat up my people as they
 eat bread? They do not call upon God.
There they were in great terror, where there was 5
 no cause for fear,
for God has scattered the bones of the men-
 pleasers; they were ashamed, for God has
 rejected them.
Who will bring about the salvation of Israel out of 6
 Zion?
When God brings back the captives of His people,
 Jacob will rejoice and Israel be glad.

PSALM 53

Save me, O God, by Your name and judge me by 1
 Your strength.
Hear my prayer, O God; give ear to the words of 2
 my mouth.

3   For insolent men have risen against me; ruthless men seek my life; they do not set God before them.
4   Behold, God is my helper; the Lord is the protector of my soul.
5   He will requite my enemies with evil; in Your truth put an end to them.
6   Voluntarily I will sacrifice to You; I will give thanks to Your name, O Lord, for it is good.
7   For You have delivered me from every trouble, and my eye has looked in triumph on my enemies!

PSALM 54

1   Give ear to my prayer, O God, and hide not Yourself from my supplication!
2   Attend to me and answer me; I am grieved in my meditation and troubled because of the noise of the enemy,
3   because of the oppression of the wicked.
    For they bring trouble upon me, and in anger they cherish enmity against me.
4   My heart is in anguish within me; the terrors of death have fallen upon me.
5   Fear and trembling come upon me, and horror overwhelms me.
6   And I say, "Oh, that I had wings like a dove! I would fly away and be at rest.

7 Yes, I would wander afar, I would lodge in the wilderness; I would hasten to find a shelter
8 from the raging wind and tempest."
9 Destroy their plans, O Lord, confuse their tongues; for I see violence and strife in the city.
10 Day and night they go around it on its walls; and mischief and trouble are within it, ruin is in its midst;
11 oppression and fraud do not depart from its marketplace.
12 It is not an enemy who taunts me—then I could bear it;
it is not an adversary who deals insolently with me—then I could hide from him.
13 But it is you, my equal, my companion, my familiar friend.
14 We used to hold sweet converse together; within God's house we walked in fellowship.
15 Let death come upon them; let them go down to Sheol alive; let them go away in terror into their graves.
16 But I call upon God, and the Lord will save me.
17 Evening and morning and at noon I utter my complaint and moan, and He will hear my voice.
18 He will deliver my soul in safety from the battle that I wage, for many are arrayed against me.
19 God will give ear and humble them, He who is before all ages.
For they suffer no calamity and therefore do not fear God.

20 My companion stretched out his hand against his friends; he violated his covenant.
21 His speech was smoother than butter, yet war was in his heart;
    his words were softer than oil, yet they were drawn swords.
22 Cast your burden on the Lord, and He will sustain you; He will never permit the righteous to be moved.
23 But You, O God, will cast them down into the lowest pit; men of blood and treachery shall not live out half their days.
    But I will trust in You.

✣ ✣ ✣

THE ORTHODOX HOME

He founded it for the joy of all the earth.
PSALM 47:2

I remember hearing that when a holy person enters a place, he or she can immediately sense its spiritual atmosphere. I have often wondered what our home feels like to a spiritual person.

As keepers of a home, we are largely responsible for that atmosphere. Not only should our homes be clean and welcoming, they should be spiritual.

Many times when my husband and I are talking to our children, we compare things we see happening at the monastery to what should be happening at home, since our homes should be a continuation of the Church. We should put into practice the things we learn, see, and feel in church—such as obedience, discipline, fasting, forgiveness, love, and prayer.

We should sprinkle prayer in every corner. Each morning, we should cense the entire house, starting with the prayer corner and making our way through the rest of the house, saying the Jesus Prayer or Psalm 141 while crossing all the icons, holy items, entryways, beds, and so forth with the censer. Many times I think of how Job would rise early to offer incense to God on behalf of his children in case they had sinned, and I too pray for the individual needs of my children, many of which are only known to God.

We should pray with every task. As we make our beds, we should pray for our husband and children, for God to watch over them and grant them peaceful and undisturbed sleep. When we wipe off our kitchen tables after a meal, we should thank God for blessing us with food to eat. While we're tidying up toys, we can ask for our children to be cheerful givers. We should always make the sign of the cross over the lunches we pack. As we pack backpacks or get school lessons ready, we should pray for God to open our children's minds and hearts to His Word and to their studies.

Fill your home with the Spirit of God. During the day, play recordings of chant or homilies and practice saying the Jesus Prayer out loud. There should be an icon in every room. Keep a Bible in a place where you know you'll open it. I keep mine on a tray by the coffee machine. It may seem like a funny place to keep a Bible, but I place it there respectfully next to a vase of flowers because one of my favorite things to do is to read while having my morning coffee. It's sort of my calm before the storm. I know that once my kids are all awake or I start working on my tasks for the day, I probably won't make time to read. You'd be surprised at how much better my days are when I start them with morning prayers and even a short reading of the Scriptures.

Set a time for prayers. Whether you're single or have a home filled with children, assigning a set time for morning and evening prayers is a must. It guarantees prayers will get done, and if you're consistently doing them at the same time each day, it will quickly become habit. Then, once prayer is a habit, you can focus on making your prayers more and more spiritual.

Have your house blessed. Most people have their homes blessed in January after Theophany, but you can have it done any time of year. If it's February, don't wait a year! A nice thing families in our church community do is to invite other families to join them. We schedule the date with our priest and then invite a few other families to share the blessing and stay for fellowship after. We have a light dessert and play board games together. It's a lot of fun.

Plan your family meals during fasting periods. This will make your life so much easier during these times. Instead of scrambling to throw meals together, you'll have a plan, and mealtimes will feel like a lot less work. No impromptu trips to the supermarket or crying in the pantry (don't judge me). The time and mental energy you save you will then be able to put toward your spiritual life.

Read spiritual books. My husband always says that reading spiritual books is like an IV for him—he always feels spiritually connected and nourished by them. He's so right. When we're reading spiritual books, somehow we're given a renewed sense of vigor and zeal. We're more eager to live spiritual lives and handle life in a better and less stressful way.

All of these things are small changes that make a big difference and will transform your house into an Orthodox home.

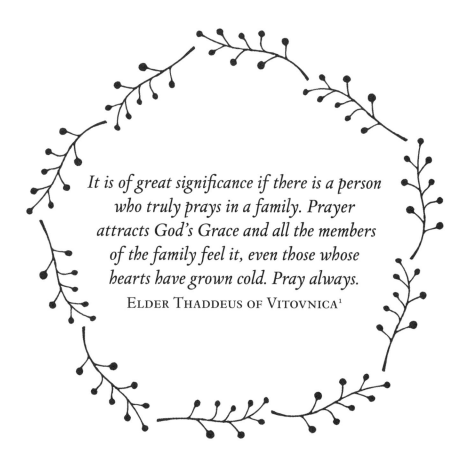

It is of great significance if there is a person who truly prays in a family. Prayer attracts God's Grace and all the members of the family feel it, even those whose hearts have grown cold. Pray always.
ELDER THADDEUS OF VITOVNICA[1]

---

1 Ana Smiljanik, *Our Thoughts Determine Our Lives: The Life and Teachings of Elder Thaddeus of Vitovnica* (Platina, CA: St. Herman of Alaska Press, 2009).

JOURNALING PAGES

KATHISMA 8

PSALM 55

1 Have mercy on me, O God, for man has trampled upon me; all day long my foe has oppressed me;
2 all day long my enemies trample upon me; many are those who fight against me.
3 In the light of day I will not fear, for I have placed my hope in the Lord.
4 In God, whose word I praise, all the day I have hoped in God; I will not fear what flesh will do to me.
5 All day long they slander my words; all their plots are against me for evil.
6 There they are; they lurk, they watch my steps; they lie in wait for my soul.
7 But You will not grant them victory; in Your wrath You will cast down the peoples, O God.
8 I have manifested my life to You; You have put my tears before You according to Your promise!
9 My enemies will be turned back in the day when I call on You; lo, I know that You are my God.
10 In God, whose word I praise, in the Lord, whose word I praise, in God I have hoped.
11 I will not be afraid of what man will do to me.
12 I will render to You, O God, the vows of praise which are upon me.

13   For You have delivered my soul from death,
>yes, my feet from falling, that I may be well-pleasing before God in the land of the living.

PSALM 56

1   Be merciful to me, O God, be merciful to me, for my soul has trusted in You;
>in the shadow of Your wings I will seek refuge till the storms of lawlessness pass by.
2   I will cry to God Most High, the God who is my benefactor.
3   He sent from heaven and saved me. He put to shame those who trampled upon me.
4   I lay down to sleep in torment, but God sent forth His mercy and His truth and delivered my soul from the midst of young lions.
>The sons of men, their teeth are spears and arrows, their tongue a sharp sword.
5   Be exalted, O God, above the heavens, and Your glory over all the earth!
6   They set a net for my steps; they bowed down my soul.
>They dug a pit before my face, but they fell into it themselves.
7   My heart, O God, is ready, my heart is ready. I will sing, yes, I will sing psalms!
8   Awake, O my soul! Awake, O harp and lyre! I will awake the dawn!
9   I will confess You, O Lord, among the peoples;
>I will sing praises to You among the nations.

For Your mercy is higher than the heavens, and 10
    Your truth reaches to the clouds.
Be exalted, O God, above the heavens, and Your 11
    glory over all the earth!

PSALM 57

Do you indeed judge according to righteousness? 1
    Do you judge rightly, O sons of men?
For in your hearts you work evils in the earth; 2
    your hands weave unrighteousness.
The wicked have gone astray from the womb; they 3
    err from their birth, speaking lies.
Their anger is like that of the serpent, like the 4
    deaf adder that stops its ear
so that it does not hear the voice of enchanters or 5
    of the charm prepared cunningly by the wise.
God has broken the teeth in their mouths; God 6
    has torn out the fangs of the young lions.
Let them vanish like water that runs away; He 7
    shall bend His bow until they fail.
They shall be as melted wax; fire has come down 8
    on them, and they no longer see the sun.
Sooner than your thorns can feel the heat, He will 9
    swallow you up alive in His wrath!
The righteous will rejoice when he sees the 10
    vengeance on the ungodly; he will bathe his
    feet in the blood of the wicked.
A man will say, "Surely, then, there is a reward for 11
    the righteous; surely there is a God who judges
    them on earth."

PSALM 58

1 Deliver me from my enemies, O God; save me from those who rise up against me.
2 Deliver me from those who work evil, and save me from bloodthirsty men.
3 For lo, they have hunted for my soul;
fierce men have set upon me for no transgression or sin of mine, O Lord, for no fault of mine.
4 Without evil, I ran and directed my course aright. Rouse Yourself, come to my help and see!
5 For You, O Lord God of hosts, the God of Israel, draw near to punish all the nations; spare none of those who work evil.
6 Each evening they come back, howling like dogs and prowling about the city.
7 There they are, bellowing with their mouths, and a sword is on their lips, for they think, "Who has heard?"
8 But You, O Lord, will laugh them to scorn; You will hold all the nations to be nothing.
9 O my strength, I shall keep watch with you, for You, O God, are my helper, and Your mercy shall go before me.
10 My God will show me my enemies; slay them not, lest they forget Your law.
11 Scatter them by Your power and bring them down, O Lord, my defender!
12 For the sin of their mouths, the words of their lips, let them be trapped in their pride.

For the cursing and lies which they utter, consume them in wrath; 13
consume them till they are no more, that they may know that the God of Jacob rules to the ends of the earth.
Each evening they come back, howling like dogs and prowling about the city. 14
They roam about for food and growl if they do not get their fill. 15
But I will sing of Your might; I will sing aloud of Your mercy in the morning. 16
For You have been my defender and my refuge in the day of my distress.
O My Helper, I will sing praises to You, O my God, for You are my defender, the God who shows me mercy. 17

PSALM 59

O God, You have rejected and destroyed us; You have been angry; yet You showed us mercy! 1
You have made the earth to quake, You have troubled it; repair its breaches, for it totters! 2
You have made Your people suffer hard things; You have given us wine to drink that made us reel. 3
You have set up a banner for those who fear You to rally to it from the bow. 4
That Your beloved may be delivered, save by Your right hand and hear me! 5

6 God has spoken in His sanctuary: "I will be exalted, and will divide up Shechem, and portion out the valley of Succoth.
7 Gilead is Mine and Manasseh is Mine; Ephraim is the protection of My head; Judah is My king.
8 Moab is My washbasin; upon Edom I will cast My shoe; the Philistines are subjected to Me."
9 Who will bring me to the fortified city? Who will lead me to Edom?
10 Will not You, O God, although You have rejected us? Will not You, O God, go forth with our armies?
11 Oh, grant us help in times of tribulation, for vain is the help of man!
12 With God we shall do valiantly; it is He who will bring our foes down to nothing.

PSALM 60

1 Hear my cry, O Lord; listen to my prayer;
2 from the ends of the earth, I cried unto You when my heart was troubled.
3 You lifted me up on a rock; You guided me, for You were my hope, a strong tower against the face of the enemy.
4 I will dwell in Your tabernacle forever; I will shelter under the shadow of Your wings!
5 For You, O God, have heard my prayers.
You have given an inheritance, O Lord, to them that fear Your name.

You will prolong the life of the king; may his years 6
  endure to all generations!
He will be enthroned forever before God. 7
Who will seek out His mercy and truth?
So will I ever sing praises to Your name, that I 8
  may pay my vows day after day.

PSALM 61

Shall not my soul be subjected to God? For from 1
  Him comes my salvation.
He only is my God and my Savior, my helper; I 2
  shall not be greatly moved.
How long will you set upon a man to shatter him, 3
  all of you, like a leaning wall, a tottering fence?
They plotted to thrust down my honor; they take 4
  pleasure in falsehood.
They blessed with their mouths, but in their
  hearts they cursed.
Nevertheless, O my soul, be subjected to God, for 5
  from Him comes patience.
He only is my God and my Savior, my helper; I 6
  shall not be moved.
On God rests my salvation and my glory, the God 7
  of my help; my hope is in God.
Hope in Him, O assembly of the people; pour out 8
  your heart before Him, for God is our helper.
But the sons of men are vain, the sons of men are a 9
  delusion; in the balances they are false; they are
  all alike vanity.

10 Put no confidence in extortion; set no vain hopes on robbery; if wealth increases, set not your heart on it.
11 Once God has spoken; twice have I heard this:
12 that power belongs to God, and that to You, O Lord, belongs mercy.
For You requite everyone according to his works.

PSALM 62

1 O God, You are my God; I seek You, my soul thirsts for You;
my flesh faints for You, as in a dry and weary land where no water is.
2 So I have looked upon You in the sanctuary, beholding Your power and glory.
3 Because Your steadfast love is better than life, my lips will praise You.
4 So I will bless You as long as I live; I will lift up my hands and call on Your name.
5 My soul is feasted as with marrow and fat, and my mouth praises You with joyful lips
6 when I think of You upon my bed and meditate on You in the watches of the night.
7 For You have been my help, and in the shadow of Your wings I sing for joy.
8 My soul clings to You; Your right hand upholds me.
9 But those who seek to destroy my life shall go down into the depths of the earth;

they shall be given over to the power of the sword; 10
 they shall be prey for jackals.
But the king shall rejoice in God; 11
all who swear by Him shall glory; for the mouths
 of liars will be stopped.

PSALM 63

Hear my voice, O God, when I pray to You; 1
 deliver my soul from dread of the enemy.
You have hidden me from the secret plots of the 2
 wicked, from the crowd of evildoers,
who whet their tongues like swords, who have 3
 bent their bow with malice,
shooting from ambush at the blameless, shooting 4
 at him suddenly and without fear.
They have set up for themselves an evil purpose; 5
 they talk of laying snares secretly;
they have said, "Who will see them?" They have
 sought out lawlessness.
They have wearied themselves with searching 6
 cunningly.
A man shall come forth whose heart is deep, and 7
 God will be exalted.
Their shafts became as children's arrows; their words 8
 were of no effect and even turned against them.
Then all men were in fear; they told what God has 9
 wrought and understood what He has done.
The righteous will rejoice in the Lord and shall 10
 set his hope on Him.
Let all the upright in heart glory.

REFUGE

*In the shadow of Your wings I will seek refuge
till the storms of lawlessness pass by.*
PSALM 56:1

God is everywhere. In our most spiritual moments, we feel His presence completely envelop us. We know without a doubt that He is near. But on those days when our patience has run low and our passions gurgle up to the surface, we need an anchor to keep us from being swallowed by the sea of life.

When storms threaten to take me under, I seek refuge at the monasteries near our home. It's there that I find the strength and encouragement I need to continue fighting through the waves. The monasteries are a port in the storm, and the monastics that sanctify their grounds are the lighthouses that guide us to safety.

My first visit to a monastery was almost twenty years ago. I was nervous, excited, and totally unprepared for what awaited me—discovering a part of my spiritual life that I didn't even know was missing.

Even though I had grown up very involved in the Church, there were certain elements of Orthodoxy that I'd never encountered until then—things like headcoverings, prostrations, and the constant practice of the Jesus Prayer. It felt as if I had stepped back in time and entered an alternate Orthodox universe. There I was, standing in this beautiful place of worship, lit only by the soft glow of vigil lamps and several thin beeswax candles. The chanting was like something straight from Paradise, and I kept catching myself closing my eyes as if trying to breathe the very breath of it deep into my soul. Black figures moved swiftly and almost silently, except for the swooshing of their monastic robes and the soft whisper of prayer on their lips.

I think perhaps the biggest surprise of all was the monastics themselves. They were nothing like the remote, stern, and silent figures I'd expected. It turned out they were just regular people who laughed and joked and had personality quirks. The only difference between them and the lay Christians I knew, other than the joy that radiated from them, was that they loved Christ in a very real-life way that I'd never even known was possible. Their love for God and His Church and the way they cared and prayed for the whole world left me in awe. And the more we visited and got to know them, the more in awe of them I was—and still am, nearly two decades later.

If you visit Orthodox countries such as Greece, Russia, Serbia, or Romania, you will find monasteries are a normal part of the landscape and a vital part of Orthodox life. But here in the United States, they were almost nonexistent until the nineties. If you've never visited a monastery, I encourage you to take a spiritual pilgrimage to the one closest to your home, even if that's not so close. I promise it will be worth the journey.

There's an old saying, "If you want to know if someone loves Christ, find out if he loves monasticism." The monasteries are a tower of strength in our weak, politically correct society, a place for us to see a living part of our Orthodox heritage that has not yielded to the spirit of the times.

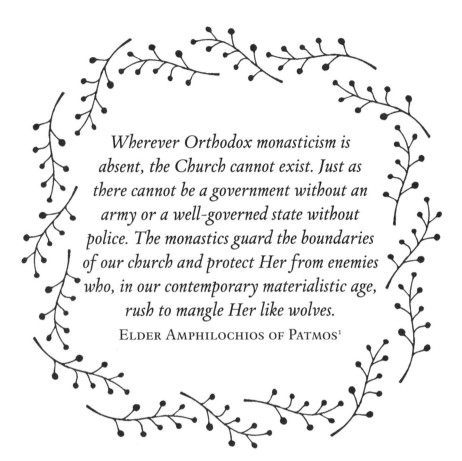

Wherever Orthodox monasticism is absent, the Church cannot exist. Just as there cannot be a government without an army or a well-governed state without police. The monastics guard the boundaries of our church and protect Her from enemies who, in our contemporary materialistic age, rush to mangle Her like wolves.
ELDER AMPHILOCHIOS OF PATMOS[1]

---

1 Herman A. Middleton, *Precious Vessels of the Holy Spirit: The Lives and Counsels of Contemporary Elders of Greece* (Protecting Veil Press, 2003), p. 52.

JOURNALING PAGES

KATHISMA 9

PSALM 64

Praise is due to You, O God, in Zion; and to You shall vows be performed. 1
Hear my prayer; to You shall all flesh come. 2
The words of transgressors have led us astray, but pardon our sins. 3
Blessed are those whom You have chosen and taken to Yourself, O Lord; they shall dwell in Your courts. 4
We shall be satisfied with the goodness of Your house; holy is Your temple, wonderful in righteousness.
Hear us, O God our Savior, the hope of all the ends of the earth, and of those who are far off beyond the sea; 5
for by Your strength You established the mountains, being girded with might; 6
You trouble the depths of the seas, the roaring of their waves. 7
The peoples shall be troubled, and those who dwell at earth's farthest bounds will be afraid at Your signs; 8
You will make the outgoings of the morning and the evening to shout for joy.
You have visited the earth and watered it; You greatly enrich it. 9

The river of God is full of water; You provide
   their grain, for so You have prepared it.
10 Water its furrows abundantly; multiply its fruits;
   send forth gentle showers upon the earth, that
   it may rejoice and bear fruit.
11 You will bless the seasons of the year with Your
   goodness; Your fields shall be filled with
   fatness.
12 The pastures of the desert will be lush and green,
   and the hills shall gird themselves with joy;
13 the meadows shall clothe themselves with flocks,
   the valleys shall deck themselves with grain;
they shall shout and sing together for joy!

PSALM 65

1 Make a joyful noise to God, all the earth!
2 Sing of His name; give glory to His praise!
3 Say to God, "How awesome are Your deeds! So
   great is Your power that Your enemies cringe
   before You."
4 Let all the earth worship You and praise You. Let
   it praise Your name, O Most High!
5 Come and see what God has done: He is terrible in
   His counsels among the sons of men.
6 He turns the sea into dry land; men will pass
   through the river on foot; there will we rejoice
   in Him.
7 He rules by His might forever; His eyes keep
   watch on the nations; let not those who provoke
   Him exalt themselves.

8 Bless our God, O peoples; make the sound of His praise be heard,
9 who keeps my soul among the living and does not let my feet slip.
10 For You, O God, have tested us; You have tried us with fire as silver is tried.
11 You brought us into the net; You laid affliction on our backs; You let men ride over our heads;
12 we went through fire and through water, yet You have brought us forth to a place of refreshment.
13 I will go into Your house with whole burnt offerings;
14 I will pay You my vows, that which my lips uttered and my mouth promised when I was in trouble.
15 I will offer to You whole burnt offerings full of marrow, with incense and rams; I will make an offering to You of bulls and goats.
16 Come and hear, all who fear God, and I will tell what He has done for my soul.
17 I cried aloud to Him with my mouth, and He was extolled with my tongue.
18 If I have cherished iniquity in my heart, let the Lord not listen to me.
19 But truly God has listened; He has given heed to the voice of my prayer.
20 Blessed be God, because He has not rejected my prayer or removed His mercy from me!

✠ ✠ ✠

PSALM 66

1 O God, be bountiful to us and bless us!
Shine the light of Your countenance upon us and
have mercy on us,
2 that we may know Your way upon the earth and
Your salvation among all nations.
3 Let the peoples give thanks to You, O God; let all
the peoples give thanks to You!
4 Let the nations be glad and sing for joy, for You
judge the peoples with equity and guide the
nations upon the earth.
5 Let the peoples give thanks to You, O God; let all
the peoples give thanks to You!
6 The earth has yielded its fruit; let God, our God,
bless us.
7 Let God bless us, and let all the ends of the earth
fear Him!

PSALM 67

1 Let God arise; let His enemies be scattered; let
those who hate Him flee from before His Face!
2 As smoke vanishes, so let them vanish—as wax
melts before the fire.
3 So the sinners will perish before the Face of God,
but let the righteous be glad.
Let them exult before God; let them be jubilant
with joy!

Sing to God, sing praises to His name; lift up a song to Him who rides upon the clouds; the Lord is His name, exult before Him!	4
They shall be troubled before the Face of Him who is Father of the fatherless and judge of the widows: so is God in His holy habitation.	5
God gives the desolate a home to dwell in; He leads out prisoners with strength, even the rebellious who dwell in the tombs.	6
O God, when You went forth before Your people, when You marched through the wilderness,	7
the earth quaked, yes, the heavens poured down rain before the Face of the God of Sinai, before the Face of the God of Israel.	8
O God, You will grant Your inheritance a gracious rain; You restored it as it languished;	9
Your flock found a dwelling in it; in Your goodness, O God, You provide for the poor.	10
The Lord God will give His Word to those proclaiming the good news with great power.	11
The king of the Beloved's armies will divide the spoil for the beauty of the house.	12
Even if you stay among the sheepfolds, you will have the wings of a dove covered with silver, its breast with gleaming gold.	13
When the Most High places kings about it, they will be made white as snow on Zalmon.	14
The mountain of God is a fertile mountain, a mountain rich like curdled milk—a rich mountain.	15
Why do you look with envy at other rich mountains?	16

This is the mountain God desired for His abode,
yes, where the Lord will dwell until the end.

17 The chariots of God are ten thousand, thousands of those who rejoice.
The Lord is among them on Sinai, in the holy place.

18 You ascended on high, leading captivity captive,
and gave gifts to men, even to the rebellious, that You might dwell among them.

19 Blessed be the Lord God; blessed be the Lord from day to day, and may the God of our salvation prosper us,

20 for He is our God, the God of salvation; and to God the Lord belongs escape from death.

21 But God will shatter the heads of His enemies, the hairy crown of those who walk in their guilty ways.

22 The Lord said, "I will bring them back from Bashan; I will bring them back from the depths of the sea

23 that you may bathe your feet in blood, that the tongues of your dogs may have their portion from the foe."

24 We have seen Your processions, O God, the processions of my God, the King, into the sanctuary:

25 the princes in front of those who play instruments, between the maidens playing timbrels.

26 Bless God in the congregations; the Lord, O you who are of Israel's fountain.

27 There is Benjamin, the younger of them, in ecstasy; the princes of Judah, their rulers; the princes of Zebulun, the princes of Naphtali.
28 Summon Your might, O God; strengthen, O God, what You have wrought for us.
29 Because of Your temple at Jerusalem, kings will bear gifts to You.
30 Rebuke the beasts that dwell among the reeds, the herd of bulls with the heifers of the peoples, lest they shut out those who have been proved like silver: scatter the peoples who delight in war.
31 Men of prayer shall come from Egypt; Ethiopia shall hasten to stretch out her hands readily to God.
32 Sing to God, O kingdoms of the earth; sing psalms to the Lord.
33 Sing to God, who rides on the heaven of heavens toward the east; lo, He sends forth His resounding voice, a mighty voice.
34 Ascribe glory to God! His majesty is over Israel, and His power is in the clouds!
35 God is glorious in His saints, the God of Israel! He gives power and strength to His people; blessed be God!

PSALM 68

1 Save me, O God! For the waters have come up to my neck.

2   I am sunk in deep mire, where there is no
      foothold; I have come into the depths of the
      sea, and a storm sweeps over me.
3   I am weary with my crying; my throat has become
      hoarse; my eyes have grown dim with waiting
      for my God.
4   More in number than the hairs of my head are
      those who hated me without a cause;
    my enemies who would persecute me
      unrighteously are strengthened;
      what I did not owe, they made me repay.
5   O God, You know my folly; the wrongs I have
      done are not hidden from You.
6   Let not those who hope on You be put to shame
      through me, O Lord God of hosts;
    let not those who seek You be brought to dishonor
      through me, O God of Israel.
7   For it is for Your sake that I have borne reproach,
      that shame has covered my face.
8   I became a stranger to my brethren, a foreigner to
      my mother's sons.
9   For zeal for Your house has consumed me, and the
      insults of those who insulted You have fallen
      on me.
10 When I humbled my soul with fasting, it became
      my reproach.
11 When I made sackcloth my clothing, I became a
      byword to them.
12 I am the talk of those who sit in the gate, and the
      drunkards make songs about me.

13 But as for me, through my prayer I remain close to You, O Lord; it is time to show Your good will, O God.

In the abundance of Your mercy hear me, in the truth of Your salvation.

14 Rescue me from sinking in the mire; let me be delivered from those who hate me and from the deep waters.

15 Let not the flood drown me, or the deep swallow me up, or the pit close its mouth over me.

16 Hear me, O Lord, for Your mercy is good; according to the abundance of Your compassion, look upon me.

17 Turn not away Your Face from Your servant, for I am afflicted.

18 Hear me speedily; attend to my soul and deliver it; deliver me because of my enemies!

19 For You know that I am reproached, covered with shame and dishonored; all who afflict me are before You.

20 My soul came to expect reproach and misery.

I looked for one to grieve with me, but there was none, and for one to comfort me, but I found none.

21 They gave me gall for food, and for my thirst they gave me vinegar to drink.

22 Let their table before them become a snare, a just retribution and a stumbling block.

23 Let their eyes be darkened so that they should not see, and bow down their backs continually.

24 Pour out Your wrath upon them, and let the fury of Your anger take hold of them.

25 May their habitation be a desolation; let no one dwell in their tents.
26 For they persecute him whom You have smitten, and they have added to the grief of my wounds.
27 Let them add iniquity to their iniquity, that they may have no access to Your justice.
28 Let them be blotted out of the book of the living; let them not be enrolled among the righteous.
29 But I am poor and afflicted; let Your salvation, O God, help me.
30 I will praise the name of my God with a song; I will magnify Him with praise.
31 This will please God more than a bull with horns and hoofs.
32 The poor see and rejoice; seek the Lord, and your soul shall live.
33 For the Lord hears the poor and does not despise His own that are in bonds.
34 Let the heavens and the earth praise Him, the seas and all things that move in them.
35 For God will save Zion, and the cities of Judah will be rebuilt;
36 His servants shall dwell there and will inherit it; the children of His servants shall possess it, and those who love His name shall dwell in it.

PSALM 69

1 Be pleased, O Lord, to deliver me; O Lord, make haste to help me!

Let them be put to shame and confusion who seek my life. 2

Let them be turned back and brought to dishonor who desire my hurt. 3

Let them be appalled because of their shame who say, "Aha! Aha!" 4

May all who seek You rejoice and be glad in You! May those who love Your salvation say evermore, "God is great!" 5

But I am poor and needy; hasten to me, O God! 6
You are my help and deliverer; O Lord, do not delay.

✠ ✠ ✠

SEEK HIM IN THE WILDERNESS

Let the heavens and the earth praise Him,
the seas and all things that move in them.
PSALM 68:34

As a child, I grew up camping. While my brother and sister dug holes in the ground with their bare hands in search of forest treasures, I was more content sitting under a tree reading a book or tying dandelion bracelets. On the rare occasion when I did venture with them into the great unknown in search of critters and mushrooms, I charged myself with the reading of the field guide, while they did all the actual fielding.

Yet, despite my reluctance to get my hands dirty, I have always loved the outdoors. There's something about being out in the middle of the woods that I was drawn to from girlhood. I love to listen to the sounds around me and watch the sunshine poke its way through the trees.

My husband, Niko, had never been camping in his life, so when we finally decided to go as a family, he was more than excited to test his outdoorsman skills with the boys. He got them new boots, compasses, and pocket knives while I created campfire menus and googled recipes for chemical-free bug repellant. We're a match made in heaven, I know.

A couple of other families joined us, and we loaded up our caravan and headed for the campground. We all agreed to turn off our cell phones and spend the weekend completely unplugged.

While preparing our site, I was surprised by the things that triggered my memories: the way the inside of the tent smelled, wearing jelly shoes in the shower, and the weird cuteness of soap-on-a-rope.

One of the other families that came brought a trifold frame with icons of the Theotokos, St. Nicholas, and Prophet Elias, which they hung on a tree in the middle of our campsites.

The first morning we were there, I woke up and went outside. The kids were still sleeping, and everyone else was either still in their tents or fumbling around in their bags. Niko had coffee made, so I poured a cup and sat at the picnic table. I let out a deep breath and closed my eyes as the warmth of my mug permeated through my hands up into my shoulders. The crisp morning air mingled with the morning sunlight and became a balm for my weary soul.

The first thing I noticed when I opened my eyes was the way the light was reflecting off the icon of the Theotokos. There was something so peaceful and serene about the look on her face, and the sun's rays seemed to bring it to life. Any worries or concerns I had melted away, and for the first time in a long time, my whole body relaxed—even my brain, which was miraculous.

Time somehow slowed down and made room for deeper thought and reflection. When you're out in the wilderness, there are no distractions. You can't worry about the laundry because there's no washing machine, and you can't fret about what you're going to make for supper because what's in the cooler is what you've got. And if you're doing it right, you also can't waste time on electronic devices because you've hidden them somewhere out of reach. It was a very liberating feeling.

By the end of the weekend, we were all rejuvenated, both mentally and spiritually. There is something about being in the great outdoors that immediately makes you feel closer to God.

Many times we read about saints, such as St. John the Baptist and St. Seraphim of Sarov, who left the world and went into the wilderness for a certain amount of time to reconnect with God. This wasn't a concept for them alone; it is a call to every one of us. It is a call to remind us that every so often we need to take a time-out, leave our worldly cares behind, and seek Him in the wilderness.

*Love every created thing.
From my childhood days,
I loved the world and its beauty.
I loved the woods and green gardens,
I loved the fields and all the beauty
of God's creation.
I liked to watch the shining clouds
scurrying across the blue sky.*
ST. SILOUAN THE ATHONITE[1]

---

1 Archimandrite Sophrony, *Wisdom from Mount Athos: The Writings of Staretz Silouan, 1866–1938* (Crestwood, NY: St. Vladimir's Seminary Press, 2001).

JOURNALING PAGES

KATHISMA 10

PSALM 70

1. **I**n You, O Lord, have I hoped; let me never be put to shame!
2. In Your righteousness, deliver me and rescue me; incline Your ear to me and save me!
3. Be a God of protection for me, a house of refuge in order to save me; for You are my fortress and my refuge.
4. Rescue me, O my God, from the hand of the wicked, from the grasp of the transgressor and unjust man.
5. For You, O Lord, are my support, my hope, O Lord, from my youth.
6. Upon You I have leaned from birth; You are my protector from my mother's womb. My praise is continually of You.
7. I have become as a portent to many, but You are my strong helper.
8. Let my mouth be filled with Your praise, O Lord, that I may sing of Your glory and honor all the day long.
9. Do not cast me off in the time of old age; forsake me not when my strength is spent.
10. For my enemies have spoken against me; those who watch for my soul consult together and say,

11 "God has forsaken him; pursue and lay hold of him, for there is none to deliver him."
12 O God, do not go far from me; O my God, come near to my help.
13 Let those who plot against my soul be put to shame and consumed; with scorn and disgrace may they be covered who seek my hurt.
14 But I will hope continually and will praise You yet more and more.
15 My mouth will tell openly of Your righteousness, of Your deeds of salvation all the day, for I am ignorant of the affairs of men.
16 I will go on in the might of the Lord; O Lord, I will speak of Your righteousness alone.
17 O God, from my youth You have taught me, and I still proclaim Your wonders even until I am old and advanced in years.
18 O God, do not forsake me till I proclaim Your arm to all the generations to come,
19 Your power and Your righteousness, O God, up to the highest heavens.
The mighty works You have done, O God! Who is like You?
20 You have made me see many sore troubles! Yet You turned and revived me and brought me again from the depths of the earth.
21 You increased Your greatness, and turned and comforted me, and brought me again from the depths of the earth.
22 Therefore I will also give thanks to You, O God, because of Your truth, on an instrument of psalmody;

I will sing praises to You with the harp, O Holy
    One of Israel.
My lips will rejoice when I sing of You; my soul
    also, which You have redeemed;
and my tongue will talk of Your righteous help all
    the day long,
while those who sought to do me hurt are put to
    shame and disgraced.

PSALM 71

Give the king Your judgment, O God, and Your
    righteousness to the king's son,
that he may judge Your people with righteousness
    and Your poor with justice!
Let the mountains receive peace for the people
    and the hills, righteousness.
He shall uphold the right of the poor of His
    people.
Save the children of the needy and crush the false
    accuser!
And he shall continue as long as the sun and the
    moon, forever!
He shall come down as dew upon a fleece and as
    the rain which falls upon the earth.
In his days shall righteousness flourish and peace
    abound till the moon be no more.
He shall have dominion from sea to sea and from
    the river to the ends of the earth.
The Ethiopians will bow down before him, and
    his enemies lick the dust.

10. The kings of Tarshish and of the isles will bring presents; the kings of Sheba and Seba will offer gifts.
11. And all kings will worship him, all nations serve him.
12. For he has delivered the poor from the oppressor, and the needy who had no helper.
13. He will spare the poor and needy and deliver the souls of the needy.
14. From usury and injustice he will redeem their souls, and his name will be in honor before them.
15. And he will live, and gold of Arabia shall be given to him.
   And men will pray for him continually, and all the day shall they praise him.
16. He will be a firm support on the earth and on the tops of the mountains;
   his fruit will be exalted higher than Lebanon, and they will flourish in the city like the grass of the field.
17. May his name be blessed forever! His name shall endure longer than the sun!
   All the tribes of the earth will be blessed in him; all nations will call him blessed.
18. Blessed be the Lord, the God of Israel, who alone does wondrous things.
19. Blessed be His glorious name forever; all the earth will be filled with His glory!
   Amen and Amen!

PSALM 72

How good is God to Israel, to the upright in heart! 1

But my feet were almost overthrown; my steps had almost slipped. 2

For I was envious of the transgressors when I saw the tranquility of sinners. 3

For there is no torment at their time of death; they remain firm in afflictions. 4

They are exempt from the troubles of men; they are not scourged along with them. 5

Therefore pride has possessed them; they have clothed themselves with their injustice and ungodliness. 6

Their fatness drips with injustice; they follow the desires of their hearts. 7

They have taken counsel and spoken in wickedness; loftily they have uttered unrighteousness. 8

They have set their mouths against heaven, and their tongue struts through the earth. 9

Therefore my people turn to them, since days of fullness are found with them. 10

And they say, "How can God know? Is there knowledge in the Most High?" 11

Behold, these are the sinners, those who always prosper; they have possessed wealth. 12

And I said, "Have I in vain kept my heart clean and washed my hands in innocence?" 13

14 For all the day long was I stricken, and chastened every morning.
15 If I had said, "I will speak thus," I would have broken covenant with the generation of Your children.
16 So I thought how to understand this;
17 it was for me a wearisome task, until I went into the sanctuary of God and I perceived their end.
18 Truly, for their crafty dealings You set a judgment for them; You cast them down when they were lifted up.
19 How they have become desolate! Suddenly they have failed; they have perished because of their iniquity.
20 They are like a dream when one awakes; O Lord, You have wiped out their image from Your city.
21 My heart burned, and my reins were troubled;
22 I was brutish and ignorant; I was like a beast before You.
23 Nevertheless I am continually with You; You have held my right hand.
24 You have guided me with Your counsel, and You have taken me to Yourself with glory.
25 For whom have I in heaven but You? And what have I desired upon earth besides You?
26 My flesh and my heart have failed, but God is the strength of my heart and my portion forever.
27 For lo, those who remove themselves far from You shall perish; You put an end to those who commit adultery against You.
28 But for me, my fullness is to cling to God, to put my trust in the Lord God, that I may proclaim

Your praises in the gates of the daughter of Zion!

PSALM 73

O God, why do You cast us off forever? Why does Your anger smoke against the sheep of Your pasture? 1

Remember Your congregation which You have gotten of old! 2
You delivered the scepter of Your inheritance, Mount Zion where You have dwelt.

Continually lift up Your hands against their pride, against all that the enemy has done wickedly in Your sanctuary. 3

Those who hate You have boasted in the midst of Your feast; 4
they have set up their own emblems on the doorposts, in place of ours, without knowing what they were doing. 5

As one fells trees in a forest with axes, they have broken down its doors; they have broken them down with axe and hammer. 6

They have burnt Your sanctuary to the ground; they desecrated the dwelling place of Your name. 7

They and all their acquaintances together have said in their hearts, "Come, let us abolish the feasts of the Lord from the face of the earth." 8

We do not see our emblems; there is no longer any prophet; and no one will recognize us anymore. 9

10 How long, O God, is the foe to scoff? Is the enemy to revile Your name forever?
11 Why do You turn back Your hand, Your right hand, from Your bosom forever?
12 Yet God is our King before the ages; He has worked salvation in the midst of the earth!
13 You established the sea by Your might; You broke the heads of the dragons in the waters.
14 You crushed the heads of the dragon; You gave him for food to the nations of Ethiopia.
15 You cut open springs and brooks; You dried up ever-flowing rivers.
16 Yours is the day, Yours also the night; You have established the luminaries and the sun.
17 You have fixed all the bounds of the earth; You have made summer and winter.
18 Remember: The enemy has reproached the Lord, and a foolish people reviles Your name.
19 Do not deliver to the wild beasts a soul that gives praise to You; do not forget the life of Your poor forever.
20 Look upon Your covenant, for the dark places of the land are full of the habitations of violence.
21 Let not the afflicted and shamed be rejected; the poor and needy shall praise Your name.
22 Arise, O God, plead Your cause; remember the insults uttered against You by the fool all the day long.
23 Do not forget the cry of Your supplicants, for the pride of those who hate You goes up continually!

PSALM 74

1 We will give thanks to You, O God; we give thanks and call on Your name; I will recount Your wondrous deeds.
2 "At the set time which I appoint, I will judge with equity.
3 The earth is dissolved, and all its inhabitants. I keep steady its pillars."
4 I say to the transgressors, "Do not transgress," and to the sinners, "Do not lift up your horn.
5 Do not lift up your horn on high or speak unrighteousness against God,
6 for salvation comes not from the east or from the west, and not from the desert mountains."
7 For God is the judge, putting down one and lifting up another.
8 For in the hand of the Lord there is a cup with unmixed wine, blended with spices, and He has poured it from cup to cup,
but its dregs have not been totally poured out; all the sinners of the earth shall drink them.
9 But I will rejoice forever; I will sing praises to the God of Jacob.
10 All the horns of the wicked I will cut off, but the horn of the righteous shall be exalted.

✠ ✠ ✠

PSALM 75

1. In Judah God is known; His name is great in Israel.
2. His abode has been in Salem and His dwelling place in Zion.
3. There He broke the power of the bow, the shield, the sword, and the battle.
4. You shine forth wondrously from the everlasting mountains.
5. All those whose hearts are without understanding were troubled; they slept their sleep and found nothing left in their hands—those who were greedy for wealth.
6. At Your rebuke, O God of Jacob, the riders on the horses slumbered.
7. But You are terrible! Who can stand before You? Your anger has been known from of old.
8. You caused judgment to be heard from heaven; the earth feared and was still
9. when God arose to establish judgment, to save all the meek in heart.
10. Therefore, the inward thought of man shall confess You, and the remembrance of it shall be as a feast.
11. Pray and make Your vows before the Lord our God; all who are around Him shall bring gifts to Him who is to be feared,
12. who cuts off the spirit of princes, who is terrible to the kings of the earth!

PSALM 76

1. I cried aloud to God with my voice; my voice cried aloud to God, and He heard me.
2. In the day of my trouble, I earnestly sought the Lord; in the night my hands were stretched out before Him, and I was not deceived; my soul refused any other consolation.
3. I remembered God, and I rejoiced; when I thought of my woes, my spirit failed.
4. My eyes were awake in vigil; I was so troubled that I could not speak.
5. I considered the days of old; I remembered the eternal years, and I meditated.
6. I labored in my heart in the night, and my spirit struggled to understand:
7. Will the Lord spurn forever and never again be favorable?
8. Has He cut off His mercy forever, from generation to generation?
9. Will God forget to be gracious? Will He in anger shut up His compassion?
10. And I said, "Now have I begun; this is the change of the right hand of the Most High."
11. I called to mind the deeds of the Lord; yes, I will remember Your wonders from the beginning.
12. I will meditate on all Your works and muse on Your deeds.
13. Your way, O God, is in holiness: Who is so great a God as our God?

14 You are the God who works wonders; You have manifested Your might among the peoples.
15 With Your arm You redeemed Your people, the sons of Jacob and Joseph.
16 The waters saw You, O God; the waters saw You and were afraid; yes, the deeps trembled.
17 There was a great sound of waters; the clouds gave forth voice; Your arrows went abroad.
18 The crash of Your thunder was in the whirlwind; Your lightning lighted up the world; the earth trembled and shook.
19 Your way is through the sea, Your paths through many waters; yet Your footprints are unknown.
20 You led Your people like sheep by the hand of Moses and Aaron.

✣ ✣ ✣

THE SO-CALLED PERFECT LIFE

I remembered God, and I rejoiced.
PSALM 76:3

So much of life is determined by perspective. The key is controlling what influences that perspective. The Holy King and Prophet David wrote in Psalm 101:3, "I will set no wicked thing before my eyes." He understood that the eyes of man were a doorway to his heart and vowed to let nothing unrighteous enter in. We must follow his example.

This means being conscious of what we see every day—whether in our real lives or our virtual ones. Women always seem to hold themselves to a (ridiculously unrealistic) standard created by the world. Why is that? Who on earth could measure up to that kind of expectation? No one. And trying to is a waste of time and a trick of the devil to divert our attention away from "the one thing needful" and toward the shiny promises of a fallen world. Personally, I refuse to chase after anything that can't add to the quality of my family's life or our salvation. If comparison is the thief of joy, than perfection is its lying accomplice.

So many people scramble through life trying desperately to create that perfect life the world tells them they deserve. Perfect appearance, perfect home, perfect spouse—anything to add to their social status. What a tiresome and empty task. These poor souls are constantly running, chasing that facade only to constantly miss the mark. Hear me: it is an unattainable goal.

Instead of working hard to gain the respect of others by bettering their character, people work hard to impress others by acquiring the most stuff. While people continue scrambling in the hunt for the so-called perfect life, their families suffer. More and more children are being raised by electronic devices and anything else that will keep them quiet.

As Orthodox Christian women living in the world, we sometimes allow our standards to become blurred. It takes constant effort to remember what God desires from us and how opposite that is from what the world wants from us. The world tells us we should have trendy wardrobes, expensive cars, and homes that look as if Joanna Gaines herself came in and did the decorating. And while sometimes, some of those things might be okay in moderation, not a single one of them will bring us or our families closer to God.

Those who continue in the hunt will wind up empty again and again, their happiness lasting only long enough for Amazon Prime to deliver their next fix. They're wasting their lives trying fill a hole inside themselves with material things instead of making room for our immaterial Christ to dwell in their hearts. Joy cannot be found in a newly decorated living room. It's not even found in the perfect handbag, and trust me, I know. True and lasting joy can only be found in Christ.

My spiritual father once told me, "Acquire joy, not happiness. Happiness is temporary, whereas joy is eternal and can only be found in Christ." Forget what makes you happy; it's fleeting. Seek what brings you joy—that is what's eternal.

Take control of the things you grant entrance into your heart. Be watchful of the things you pacify yourself with. Give thanks for the mundane and savor the simple. Most often, the most extraordinary things in our lives aren't really things at all and are hidden away in the most ordinary of days.

> *It is not from external circumstances but internal attitudes that sorrows and joys are born.*
> —St. John Chrysostom[1]

---

[1] *On Wealth and Poverty* (Crestwood, NY: St. Vladimir's Seminary Press, 1999).

JOURNALING PAGES

KATHISMA 11

PSALM 77

G̲ive ear, O my people, to my law; incline your ears to the words of my mouth! 1
I will open my mouth in parables; I will utter dark sayings from of old, 2
things that we have heard and known, that our fathers have told us. 3
They did not hide them from their children 4
so that they would tell them to the coming generation;
that they would declare the praises of the Lord and His mighty acts, and the wonders which He has wrought.
He established a testimony in Jacob and appointed a law in Israel, 5
which He commanded our fathers to make known to their children,
that the next generation might know them, the children yet unborn, 6
and arise and tell them to their children, so that they should set their hope in God 7
and not forget the works of God but observe His commandments;
that they should not be like their fathers, a stubborn and rebellious generation, 8

a generation whose heart was not steadfast, whose spirit was not faithful to God.

9 The sons of Ephraim, bending and shooting the bow, turned back on the day of battle.

10 They did not keep God's covenant and would not walk according to His law.

11 And they forgot His benefits and His miracles He had shown them,

12 the miracles He wrought in the sight of their fathers, in the land of Egypt, in the fields of Tanis.

13 He divided the sea and led them through it, and made the waters stand as in a bottle.

14 In the daytime He led them with a cloud, and all the night with a fiery light.

15 He cleft rocks in the wilderness and gave them drink abundantly as from the deep.

16 He made streams come out of the rock and caused waters to flow down like rivers.

17 Yet they sinned still more against Him, provoking the Most High in the desert.

18 They tested God in their heart by demanding the food they craved in their soul.

19 They also spoke against God, saying, "Can God spread a table in the wilderness?

20 He smote the rock so that water gushed out and streams overflowed.

Can He also give bread or prepare a table for His people?"

21 Therefore the Lord heard and was full of wrath; a fire was kindled against Jacob; His anger mounted against Israel,

because they had no faith in God and did not trust in His salvation.	22
Yet He commanded the clouds from above and opened the doors of heaven,	23
and He rained down upon them manna to eat and gave them the bread of heaven.	24
Man ate of the bread of the angels; He sent them food in abundance.	25
He raised the east wind from heaven, and by His power He led out the south wind;	26
He rained flesh upon them like dust, winged birds like the sand of the seas;	27
they fell in the midst of their camp, all around their tents.	28
And they ate and were well filled, for He gave them what they craved.	29
They were not disappointed in their desire, yet while the food was still in their mouths, the anger of God rose against them,	30
and He slew the strongest of them and laid low the picked men of Israel.	31
In spite of all this, they still sinned; they did not believe in His wonders.	32
And their days were consumed in vanity and their years in anxiety.	33
When He slew them, they sought for Him; they returned and sought God earnestly.	34
They remembered that God was their helper, the Most High God their Redeemer.	35
But they flattered Him with their mouths; they lied to Him with their tongues.	36

37 Their heart was not true toward Him; they were not steadfast in His covenant.
38 Yet He is compassionate and will forgive their sins, and will not destroy them;
yes, He will restrain His anger often and will not stir up all His wrath.
39 He remembered that they are but flesh, a wind that passes and comes not again.
40 How often they provoked Him in the wilderness and angered Him in the desert!
41 Yes, they turned back and tested God and provoked the Holy One of Israel.
42 They did not keep in mind His hand, the day when He redeemed them from the hand of the oppressor;
43 when He had wrought His signs in Egypt and His miracles in the fields of Tanis, and had turned
44 their rivers to blood, and their streams so that they could not drink.
45 He sent among them swarms of flies, which devoured them, and frogs, which destroyed them.
46 He gave their crops to the canker worm and their labors to the locust.
47 He destroyed their vines with hail and their sycamores with frost.
48 He gave over their cattle to the hail and their possessions to fire.
49 He let loose on them the fierceness of His anger, wrath, indignation, and distress, a company of destroying angels.

He made a path for His anger; He did not spare 50
their souls from death, but gave even their
cattle over to death.

He smote every firstborn in the land of Egypt, the 51
first fruits of their labors in the tents of Ham.

And He led out His people like sheep and guided 52
them in the wilderness like a flock.

And He guided them with hope, so that they were 53
not afraid; but the sea covered their enemies.

And He brought them to the mountain of His 54
holiness, this mountain which His right hand
had won.

He drove out nations before them; He apportioned 55
for them an inheritance by line and settled the
tribes of Israel in their tents.

Yet they tested and provoked the Most High God 56
and did not observe His testimonies.

And they turned away and broke covenant like 57
their fathers; they became like a twisted bow.

And they provoked Him to wrath with their high 58
places; they moved Him to jealousy with their
graven images.

God heard and despised them, and He utterly 59
rejected Israel.

He rejected the tabernacle at Shiloh, His tent 60
where He dwelt among men,

and delivered their power into captivity, their 61
beauty to the hand of the foe.

He gave His people over to the sword and despised 62
His heritage.

Fire devoured their young men, and their maidens 63
were not mourned.

64 Their priests fell by the sword, and their widows were not lamented.
65 Then the Lord awoke as one from sleep, like a strong man excited by wine.
66 And He smote His adversaries as they fled; He put them to everlasting shame.
67 And He rejected the tabernacle of Joseph; He did not choose the tribe of Ephraim;
68 but He chose the tribe of Judah, Mount Zion
69 which He loved: He fashioned it for His holy abode, like the earth, which He has founded forever.
70 He chose David His servant and took him up from the flocks of sheep;
71 He took him from following the ewes with young to be the shepherd of Jacob His servant and Israel His inheritance.
72 And he tended them in the innocence of his heart and guided them with the skillfulness of his hands.

PSALM 78

1 O God, the nations have come into Your inheritance;
they have defiled Your holy temple; they have made Jerusalem a storage place for crops.
2 They have given the dead bodies of Your servants to the birds of the air for food, the flesh of Your saints to the beasts of the earth.

They have poured out their blood like water round about Jerusalem, and there was none to bury them.	3
We have become a taunt to our neighbors, mockery and derision to those round about us.	4
How long, O Lord? Will You be angry forever? Will Your jealous wrath burn like fire?	5
Pour out Your anger on the nations that have not known You and on the kingdoms that have not called on Your name!	6
For they have devoured Jacob and laid waste his habitation.	7
Do not remember our transgressions from of old;	8
let Your tender mercies, O Lord, speedily go before us, for we have become exceedingly poor.	
Help us, O God of our salvation, for the glory of Your name.	9
O Lord, deliver us and purge away our sins for Your name's sake, lest by chance the nations say, "Where is their God?"	10
Let the avenging of the outpoured blood of Your servants be known among the nations before our eyes!	
Let the groans of the captives come before You; according to Your great power, preserve the sons of those who were slain!	11
Return sevenfold into the bosom of our neighbors the taunts with which they have taunted You, O Lord!	12
Then we, Your people, the sheep of Your pasture, will give thanks to You forever;	13

throughout all generations, we will recount
Your praise.

PSALM 79

1 Give ear, O Shepherd of Israel, You who lead Joseph like a flock; manifest Yourself, You who sit upon the cherubim.
2 O Lord, raise up Your might before Ephraim and Benjamin and Manasseh, and come to save us!
3 Lead us back, O Lord; let Your Face shine, and we will be saved.
4 O Lord God of hosts, how long will You be angry with the prayer of Your servant?
5 How long will You feed us with the bread of tears and cause us to drink tears in full measure?
6 You have made us an object of contention to our neighbors, and our enemies have mocked us.
7 Lead us back, O Lord God of hosts; let Your Face shine, and we will be saved.
8 You brought a vine out of Egypt; You drove out the nations and planted it.
9 You made a way for it and planted its roots, and it filled the land.
10 Its shadow covered the mountains, its branches the cedars of God.
11 It sent out its branches to the sea and its shoots to the river.
12 Why then have You broken down its hedge so that all who pass along the way pluck its fruit?

13 The boar from the forest ravages it, and the wild beast has devoured it.
14 Return, O God of hosts, we pray; look down from heaven and see and visit this vine.
15 Restore what Your right hand has planted and look on the son of man, whom You have made strong for Yourself.
16 It is burnt with fire and dug up; they will perish at the rebuke of Your countenance!
17 Let Your hand be upon the man of Your right hand, on the son of man whom You have made strong for Yourself.
18 Then we will never turn back from You; You will give us life, and we will call on Your name.
19 Lead us back, O Lord God of hosts; let Your Face shine, and we will be saved.

PSALM 80

1 Rejoice in God our helper; rejoice greatly in the Living God!
2 Take up a psalm and sound the timbrel, the sweet psaltery with the harp.
3 Blow the trumpet at the new moon on this solemn day of our feast.
4 For it is a statute for Israel, an ordinance of the God of Jacob.
5 He made it a testimony in Joseph when he went out from the land of Egypt;
he heard a language he did not understand.

6 He relieved his back from forced labors, for his hands slaved in making baskets.
7 "In distress you called on Me, and I delivered you; I heard you in the secret place of the storm; I tested you at the waters of rebellion.
8 Hear, O my people, and I will speak to you, O Israel; I will testify to you:
9 If you listen to me, there shall be no new god among you;
you shall not worship a foreign god.
10 For I am the Lord your God, who brought you up out of the land of Egypt.
Open your mouth wide, and I will fill it.
11 But my people did not listen to My voice; Israel gave no heed to Me.
12 So I let them follow their own hearts; they shall go on in their own ways.
13 If My people had listened to Me, if Israel had walked in My ways,
14 I would very soon have subdued their enemies and made their oppressors feel the weight of My hand."
15 The enemies of the Lord tried to deceive Him; the time of their punishment shall be forever.
16 But He fed his own with the finest of the wheat and satisfied them with honey from the rock.

PSALM 81

1 God stands in the divine assembly; in their midst, He judges the gods!

How long will you judge unjustly and take the side 2
of sinners?
Give justice to the orphan and the destitute; 3
uphold the right of the lowly and the poor.
Rescue the poor and destitute, and deliver him out 4
of the hand of the sinner.
They have neither knowledge nor understanding: 5
they walk about in darkness; all the foundations
of the earth shall be shaken!
I have said, "You are gods, all of you sons of the 6
Most High;
but you shall die like all men and fall like any 7
prince."
Arise, O God, judge the earth: for to You belong 8
all the nations!

PSALM 82

O God, who is like unto You? Do not be silent or 1
be still, O God!
For lo, Your enemies make themselves heard; 2
those who hate You have raised their head.
They have plotted wickedly against Your people; 3
they have conspired against Your holy ones.
They have said, "Come, let us wipe them out 4
from the nations; let the name of Israel be
remembered no more!"
Yes, they conspire with one accord; against You 5
they make a covenant:
the tents of Edom and the Ishmaelites, Moab and 6
the Hagrites,

7 Gebal and Ammon and Amalek, Philistia with the inhabitants of Tyre;
8 Assyria also has joined them; they have become a help to the children of Lot.
9 Do to them as You did to Midian and to Sisera, as to Jabin at the river Kishon,
10 who were utterly destroyed at Endor, who became dung for the ground.
11 Make their princes like Oreb and Zeeb, all the princes like Zebah and Zalmunna,
12 who said, "Let us take to ourselves the altar of God as an inheritance."
13 O my God, make them like whirling dust, like chaff before the wind.
14 As fire shall burn the forest, as the flame may consume the mountains,
15 so shall You pursue them with Your tempest and terrify them with Your anger!
16 Fill their faces with shame so that they shall seek Your name, O Lord.
17 Let them be put to shame and dismayed forever; yes, let them perish in disgrace.
18 Let the nations understand that Your name is the Lord, that You alone are the Most High over all the earth.

PSALM 83

1 How lovely are Your dwelling places, O Lord of hosts!

2 My soul longs and faints for the courts of the Lord; my heart and flesh sing for joy to the living God.
3 Even the sparrow finds a home and the swallow a nest for herself where she may lay her young:
at Your altars, O Lord of hosts, my King and my God.
4 Blessed are those who dwell in Your house, ever singing Your praise!
5 Blessed are they whose strength is in You, in whose heart are the highways to Zion.
6 They shall pass through the valley of tears to the place which You appointed;
there the Lawgiver shall give blessings.
7 They will go from strength to strength; the God of gods will be seen in Zion.
8 O Lord God of hosts, hear my prayer; give ear, O God of Jacob!
9 Behold, O God our protector; look upon the face of Your Anointed!
10 For a day in Your courts is better than a thousand elsewhere.
I would rather be a doorkeeper in the house of my God than dwell in the tents of wickedness.
11 For the Lord God loves mercy and truth; He bestows grace and glory.
No good thing does the Lord withhold from those who walk uprightly.
12 O Lord of hosts, blessed is the man who trusts in You!

PSALM 84

1. You have shown favor to Your land, O Lord; You have brought back the captives of Jacob.
2. You forgave the iniquity of Your people; You pardoned all their sin.
3. You withdrew all Your wrath; You turned from Your hot anger.
4. Restore us again, O God of our salvation, and put away Your indignation toward us!
5. Will You be angry with us forever? Will You prolong Your anger to all generations?
6. O God, You will return and give us life, and Your people will rejoice in You.
7. Show us Your mercy, O Lord, and grant us Your salvation.
8. Let me hear what God the Lord will speak, for He will speak peace to His people, to His saints, to those who turn to Him in their hearts.
9. Surely His salvation is at hand for those who fear Him, that glory may dwell in our land.
10. Mercy and truth have met; righteousness and peace have kissed each other.
11. Truth arose from the earth, and righteousness looked down from the sky.
12. Yes, the Lord will pour out His sweet goodness, and our land will yield its fruit.
13. Righteousness will go before Him, and its footsteps shall open the way.

MY NEST

How lovely are Your dwelling places, O Lord of hosts!
PSALM 83:1

A woman's home is a reflection of herself. Whether we live in an enormous estate, a quaint cottage, or a tiny apartment, the atmosphere we create in our home offers a glimpse into our heart.

The secular world wants to tell us that things like keeping a home and taking pride in our housekeeping are antiquated and futile, but those of us who have found joy in these things know better than to believe that. We know what a blessed task we have in making our house a home and creating an atmosphere that our husbands can find rest in and that our children will remember all their lives. It's a tremendous responsibility, but it's also a greater blessing than we deserve.

A while ago, I posted some journaling prompts for each day of Great Lent, and one of the prompts was to list your home goals. It was one of my favorite prompts. Somehow, writing down my goals makes them feel more achievable, and it gives me a sort of game plan. When I summed up my home goals, I was surprised to realize they didn't require any sort of magical Mary Poppins skills and were actually pretty simple. I wrote:

"I want our home to be a haven of prayer and filled with the presence of God. A safe place that sounds of laughter and smells of freshly baked chocolate chip cookies and feels like a warm hug. With Small Compline after dinner and a game of Scrabble before bed."

One day, when my children are all grown up, I want them to look back at their childhoods with fondness, remembering our prayer time as a family and all the memories we made crowded around the kitchen counter or snuggled up on the couch reading a book aloud.

When guests visit our home, I hope they'll feel welcome and comfortable. I don't care if people think my house is beautiful; I just want them to feel at home. The greatest compliment someone can offer about my home is that it feels homey. That's what makes me happy.

Keeping a home in order can get overwhelming at times, so I've made a list of just a few things you can do to give your home a quick and cozy pick-me-up. These are the things I always start with when I feel overwhelmed or don't know where to start.

» Tidy up any areas that are cluttered. (Like the counter with the pile of mail you haven't had time to sort, etc.)
» Make sure your sink is empty and wiped down.
» Vacuum.
» Light a candle and add fresh flowers to your kitchen or coffee table.
» Bake something that smells delicious.

There may be plenty more to do—there usually is—but I always find that when my main areas are tidied up, I feel calmer and less overwhelmed.

If you looked at your reflection in your home, what would you see? What are your home goals?

Neither walls nor rich furniture make a home. Millionaires in magnificent mansions may never know a home. But where there are good relationships, where love binds the family together and to God, there happiness is always to be found.

ST. SERAPHIM OF SAROV

JOURNALING PAGES

KATHISMA 12

PSALM 85

Incline Your ear, O Lord, and answer me, for I am poor and needy. 1

Preserve my life, for I am godly; save Your servant who trusts in You. 2

You are my God; be gracious to me, O Lord, for to You do I cry all the day. 3

Gladden the soul of Your servant, for to You, O Lord, do I lift up my soul. 4

For You, O Lord, are good and forgiving, abounding in mercy to all who call on You. 5

Give ear, O Lord, to my prayer; hearken to my cry of supplication. 6

In the day of my trouble I call on You, for You answer me. 7

There is none like You among the gods, O Lord, nor are there any works like Yours. 8

All the nations You have made shall come and bow down before You, O Lord, and shall glorify Your Name. 9

For You are great and do wondrous things; You alone are God. 10

Lead me in Your way, O Lord, that I may walk in Your truth; let my heart find its joy in the fear of Your Name. 11

12 I give thanks to You, O Lord my God, with my whole heart, and I will glorify Your Name forever.
13 For great is Your mercy toward me; You have delivered my soul from the depths of Sheol.
14 O God, insolent men have risen up against me; a band of ruthless men seek my life, and they do not set You before them.
15 But You, O Lord, are a God compassionate and merciful, longsuffering, and abounding in mercy and truth.
16 Look upon me and take pity on me; give Your strength to Your servant and save the son of Your handmaid.
17 Set upon me a sign of salvation, that those who hate me may see and be put to shame, because You, O Lord, have helped me and comforted me.

PSALM 86

1 His foundations rest upon the holy mountains.
2 The Lord loves the gates of Zion more than all the tabernacles of Jacob.
3 Glorious things have been spoken of you, O City of God.
4 To those who know me, I will mention Rahab and Babylon;
behold also the foreigners, and Tyre, with the people of Ethiopia: all these were born there.

5 "Zion is my mother," a man will say, for such a man was born in her; and the Most High Himself has established her.
6 The Lord shall record in the Scriptures of the people and princes all those who were born in her.
7 All those whose dwelling is within you rejoice!

PSALM 87

1 O Lord, my God, I call for help by day; I cry out in the night before You.
2 Let my prayer come before You; incline Your ear to my cry!
3 For my soul is full of troubles, and my life draws near to Sheol.
4 I am reckoned among those who go down to the Pit; I am a man who has no strength,
5 like one forsaken among the dead, like the slain that lie in the grave,
like those whom You remember no more, for they are cut off from Your hand.
6 You have put me in the depths of the Pit, in the regions dark and deep.
7 Your wrath lies heavy upon me, and You overwhelm me with all Your waves.
8 You have caused my companions to shun me; You have made me a thing of horror to them.
9 I am shut in so that I cannot escape; my eyes grow dim through sorrow.

Every day I call upon You, O Lord; I spread out
   my hands to You.
10 Do You work wonders for the dead? Do the shades
   rise up to praise You?
11 Is Your steadfast love declared in the grave or
   Your faithfulness in Abaddon?
12 Are Your wonders known in the darkness or Your
   saving help in the land of forgetfulness?
13 But I, O Lord, cry to You; in the morning my
   prayer comes before You.
14 O Lord, why do You cast me off? Why do You
   hide Your Face from me?
15 Afflicted and close to death from my youth up, I
   suffer Your terrors; I am helpless.
16 Your wrath has swept over me; Your dread assaults
   destroy me.
17 They surround me like a flood all day long; they
   close in upon me together.
18 You have caused lover and friend to shun me; my
   companions are in darkness.

PSALM 88

1 I will sing of Your mercy, O Lord, forever; with
   my mouth I will proclaim Your truth to all
   generations.
2 For You have said, "Mercy will be established
   forever, and My truth will be prepared in the
   heavens.
3 I made a covenant with My chosen ones; I swore
   to David my servant,

'I will establish your seed forever and build up your throne to all generations.'"	4
The heavens praise Your wonders, O Lord, Your truth in the assembly of the saints!	5
For who in the skies can be compared to the Lord?	6
Who shall be likened to the Lord among the sons of God?	
God is glorified in the council of the saints, great and terrible toward all that are round about Him.	7
O Lord God of hosts, who is like You?	8
You are mighty, O Lord, and Your truth is round about You.	
You rule the might of the sea; You still the tumult of its waves.	9
You have humbled the proud, You have wounded him unto death,	10
and by the power of Your arm You have scattered Your enemies.	
The heavens are Yours; the earth also is Yours; You have founded the world and its fullness.	11
The north and the west, You have created them; Tabor and Hermon shall rejoice in Your name!	12
Yours is the mighty arm; let Your hand be strengthened; let Your right hand be exalted.	13
Righteousness and judgment are the foundation of Your throne; mercy and truth shall go before Your Face.	14
Blessed are the people who know the festal shout!	15

16 O Lord, they shall walk in the light of Your
      countenance and shall exult in Your name
      forever and be exalted in Your righteousness.
17 For You are the boast of their strength, and in
      Your good pleasure our horn shall be exalted.
18 For our help is from the Lord and from the Holy
      One of Israel, our King.
19 Of old, You spoke in a vision to Your sons and
      said,
    "I have laid help on one who is mighty; I have
      exalted one chosen from My people.
20 I have found David, My servant; with My holy oil
      I have anointed him;
21 for My hand shall support him, My arm shall
      strengthen him.
22 The enemy shall have no advantage against him,
      and the son of iniquity shall not hurt him.
23 And I will hew down his foes before him and put
      to flight those who hate him.
24 But My truth and My mercy shall be with him,
      and in My name shall his horn be exalted.
25 And I will set his hand on the sea and his right
      hand on the rivers.
26 He shall cry to me, 'You are my Father, my God,
      and the helper of my salvation.'
27 And I will make him the firstborn, higher than
      the kings of the earth.
28 My steadfast love I will keep for him forever, and
      My covenant will be firm for him.
29 And I will establish his seed forever and ever and
      his throne as the days of heaven.

30 If his sons forsake My law and do not walk in My judgments,
31 if they violate My statutes and do not keep My commandments,
32 then I will punish their transgressions with a rod and their sins with scourges;
33 but I will not turn away from him My mercy, nor in My truth will I bring him harm.
34 I will by no means violate My covenant or negate the word that went forth from My lips.
35 Once for all I have sworn by My holiness that I will not lie to David.
36 His seed shall endure forever and his throne as the sun before Me, like the moon that is established
37 forever: faithful witnesses in heaven."
38 Yet You have cast off and despised, You have rejected Your anointed.
39 You have overthrown the covenant of Your servant; You have defiled his sanctuary to the ground.
40 You have broken down all his hedges; You have filled his strongholds with terror.
41 All that pass by despoil him; he has become a reproach to his neighbors.
42 You have exalted the right hand of his foes; You have made all his enemies rejoice.
43 You have deprived him of the help of his sword and have not supported him in battle.
44 You have stripped him of his purity and cast his throne to the ground.
45 You have cut short his days; You have covered him with shame.

46 How long, O Lord, will You turn away? Forever? Will Your wrath burn like fire?
47 Remember what my being is. Is it for nothing that You have created all the sons of men?
48 What man shall live and not see death, and deliver his soul from the hand of Sheol?
49 O Lord, where are Your mercies of old, which in Your truth You swore to David?
50 Remember, O Lord, the offenses which many nations have committed against Your servants and which I bear in my bosom;
51 with which Your enemies taunt, O Lord, with which they mock the advent of Your anointed.
52 Blessed be the Lord forever! Amen and Amen.

PSALM 89

1 Lord, You have been our refuge from generation to generation.
2 Before the mountains were born and before the earth and the world were formed, You are from everlasting.
3 Do not turn men back to the dust and say, "Turn back, O you sons of men."
4 For a thousand years in Your sight are but as yesterday when it is past or as a watch in the night.
5 What are the years of a man? In one morning they pass away like grass:
6 in the morning it flourishes and thrives; in the evening it fades and withers.

7 For we are consumed by Your anger; by Your wrath we are overwhelmed.
8 You have set our iniquities before You, our deeds in the light of Your countenance.
9 Therefore, all our days are gone, and we have passed away under Your wrath; our years are like a spider's web.
10 The years of our life are threescore and ten, or even by reason of strength fourscore, and the greater part of them is toil and trouble; but Your kindness comes upon us, and we are thus instructed.
11 Who considers the power of Your anger and measures the vehemence of Your wrath?
12 Manifest Your right hand that we may be instructed in our hearts with wisdom.
13 Return, O Lord! How long? Have pity on Your servants.
14 Satisfy us in the morning with Your steadfast love, that we may rejoice and be glad all our days.
15 Make us glad as many days as You have afflicted us and as many years as we have seen evil.
16 Let Your work be manifest to Your servants and Your glorious power to their children.
17 Let the favor of the Lord our God be upon us and establish the work of our hands. Yes, establish the work of our hands.

✠ ✠ ✠

PSALM 90

1. He who dwells in the shelter of the Most High will abide in the shadow of the Heavenly God.
2. He will say to the Lord, "My protector and my refuge, my God, in whom I trust."
3. For He will deliver you from the snare of the fowler and from the deadly pestilence;
4. He will cover you with His pinions, and under His wings you will find refuge;
   His truth is a shield and buckler.
5. You will not fear the terror of the night, nor the arrow that flies by day,
6. nor the pestilence that stalks in darkness, nor the demon at noonday.
7. A thousand may fall at your side, ten thousand at your right hand, but it will not come near you.
8. You will only look with your eyes and see the recompense of the wicked.
9. Because you have made the Lord your refuge, the Most High your habitation,
10. no evil shall befall you, no scourge come near your tent.
11. For He will give His angels charge of you, to guard you in all your ways.
12. On their hands they will bear you up, lest you dash your foot against a stone.
13. You will tread on the asp and the basilisk; the lion and the dragon you will trample underfoot.

"Because he cleaves to Me in love, I will deliver him; I will protect him, because he knows My name. 14

When he calls to Me, I will answer him; I will be with him in trouble; I will rescue him and glorify him. 15

With long life I will satisfy him and show him My salvation." 16

✠ ✠ ✠

FIREFLIES

*I will sing of Your mercy, O Lord, forever;
with my mouth I will proclaim Your truth to all generations.*
PSALM 88:1

One of my favorite things to do with my boys in the summer is to catch lightning bugs. We poke holes through metal jar lids, then head to the backyard, where we quietly wait to see where those magical flashes of light will appear. The boys run around in the darkness, giggling and chasing those beautiful flickers of light, hoping to hold that light in their hands. Fireflies are just a tiny part of something bigger—summertime.

The Christian life is similar to this. We're asked to shine our tiny flicker of light, a gift of baptism, in the darkness that surrounds us.

If you're paying any attention at all to the rapidly declining spiritual state of this world, you know that the light of Christ is needed more now than ever. Fr. Josiah Trenham, in his podcast series *The Arena*, once said, "When the darkness gets thicker, the light must get brighter. This is what must happen."[1] This is a call to action.

In a time when oversensitivity and false love prevail, it's our duty to make sure we're living our lives as true Christians, not only to save our own souls but to help those around us see and feel the true love of Christ and be transformed by it. We have been given a rich spiritual inheritance, and it is our duty to share it with the world.

Have you ever asked yourself what you do differently from an unbeliever? How will the world know Christ if those of us who call ourselves Christians are no different from those who worship at the altar of the world?

---

1 http://www.ancientfaith.com/podcasts/thearena/shine_your_light_for_christ

As Orthodox Christians, we don't go door to door preaching our faith; we live it in our own lives and trust God to do the rest. There's a common misconception out there that Christians are supposed to be perfect. But you know what? There's no such thing. A good Christian is not perfect. A good Christian is struggling. We do our best to follow the path of Christ, but we will fall a million times along the way. What makes us different is that we have the Church to help us up each and every time we fall, through the Mystery of Confession. It's the Mysteries that turn our flickers into flames.

As time goes on, the light of Christ is needed more and more. As politically incorrect as some may try to make you feel for shining it, keep shining. Be brave and shine brightly. You never know who is standing quietly in the darkness, hoping to hold the light. If we don't answer the call, who will?

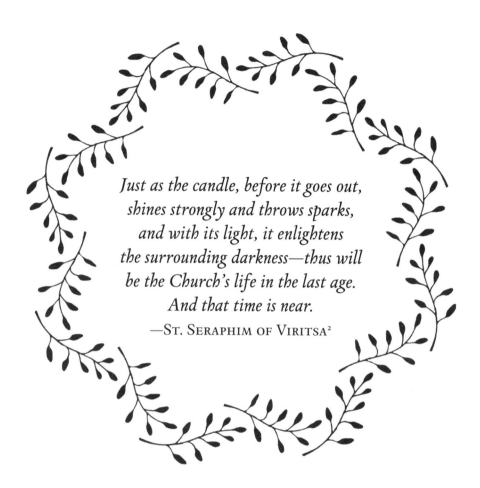

Just as the candle, before it goes out, shines strongly and throws sparks, and with its light, it enlightens the surrounding darkness—thus will be the Church's life in the last age. And that time is near.
—St. Seraphim of Viritsa[2]

---

[2] *Life – Miracles – Prophecies of Saint Seraphim of Viritsa: The New Saint of Orthodox Russian Church 1866–1949* (Thessaloniki, Greece: Orthodoxos Kypseli Publications, 2005).

JOURNALING PAGES

KATHISMA 13

PSALM 91

It is good to give thanks to the Lord, to sing praises to Your name, O Most High! 1

To declare Your mercy in the morning and Your truth by night, 2

to the music of the lute and the harp, to the melody of the lyre. 3

For You, O Lord, have made me glad by Your work; at the works of Your hands I sing for joy. 4

How great are Your works, O Lord! Your thoughts are very deep! 5

A dull man cannot know, a fool cannot understand this. 6

Though the wicked sprout like grass and all evildoers flourish, they are doomed to destruction forever. 7

But You, O Lord, are Most High forever. 8

For lo, Your enemies, O Lord, for lo, Your enemies shall perish; all evildoers shall be scattered. 9

But my horn shall be exalted like the horn of the wild bull; my old age shall be strengthened by Your anointing. 10

My eyes have seen the downfall of my enemies, and my ears have heard the doom of my evil assailants. 11

12 The righteous flourish like the palm tree and grow like a cedar in Lebanon.
13 They are planted in the house of the Lord; they flourish in the courts of our God.
14 Their old age shall be fruitful, and they shall be ever full of vigor,
15 to declare that the Lord our God is righteous, and there is no unrighteousness in Him.

PSALM 92

1 The Lord is King; He is robed in majesty. The Lord is robed; He is girded with strength.
For He has established the world so that it shall never be moved.
2 Your throne is prepared from of old; You are from everlasting.
3 The rivers have lifted up, O Lord, the rivers have lifted up their voice;
4 the rivers lift up their waves at the roaring of many waters.
Mighty are the waves of the sea; the Lord on high is mighty.
5 Your testimonies are very sure; holiness befits Your house, O Lord, forevermore!

PSALM 93

1 The Lord is a God of vengeance; the God of vengeance will act with boldness.

Arise, O Judge of the earth: render a reward to the proud! 2

How long shall sinners, O Lord, how long shall sinners boast? 3

How long will they utter and speak unrighteousness; how long will all the workers of iniquity lift up their voice? 4

They have afflicted Your people, O Lord, and oppressed Your heritage. 5

They have slain the widow and the orphan and murdered the foreigner. 6

And they said, "The Lord will not see; the God of Jacob will not perceive." 7

Understand now; O you simple among the people and fools, finally be wise. 8

He who planted the ear, does He not hear? Or He who formed the eye, does He not see? 9

He who admonishes the nations, shall He not chastise—He who teaches man knowledge? 10

The Lord knows the thoughts of men, that they are vain. 11

Blessed is the man whom You will instruct, O Lord, and will teach out of Your law, 12

to give him respite from evil days until a pit is dug for the wicked. 13

For the Lord will not forsake His people; He will not abandon His inheritance 14

until judgment again becomes righteous and all the upright in heart follow it. 15

Who will rise up for me against the transgressors? Or who will stand up for me against the workers of iniquity? 16

17 If the Lord had not helped me, my soul would already have dwelt in Sheol.
18 When I said, "My foot slips," Your mercy, O Lord, came to my help.
19 O Lord, in the same measure as the grief within my heart, Your consolations filled my soul with joy.
20 Shall the throne of the wicked have fellowship with You, the throne which makes mischief a statute?
21 They will hunt for the soul of the righteous and condemn innocent blood.
22 But the Lord was my refuge, and my God the foundation of my hope.
23 And He will bring back on them their iniquity and their wickedness: the Lord our God will wipe them out.

PSALM 94

1 Come, let us rejoice in the Lord! Let us make a joyful noise to God our Savior!
2 Let us come before His Face with thanksgiving; let us make a joyful noise to Him with psalms!
3 For the Lord is a great God and a great King over all the earth.
4 For in His hands are the depths of the earth; the heights of the mountains are His also.
5 For the sea is His, for He made it; for His hands formed the dry land.

Come, let us worship and fall down before Him and weep before the Lord our Maker!	6
For He is our God, and we are the people of His pasture and the sheep of His hand.	7
Today, if you will hear His voice, harden not your hearts, as in the rebellion, in the day of trial in the wilderness,	8
where your fathers tested Me, tried Me, and saw My works forty years.	9
Therefore I was angry with that generation and said, "They always go astray in their hearts, and they have not known my ways."	10
So I swore in my wrath, "They shall not enter My rest."	11

PSALM 95

Sing to the Lord a new song; sing to the Lord, all the earth!	1
Sing to the Lord, bless His name; from day to day, proclaim the salvation of our God.	2
Declare His glory among the nations, His marvelous works among all peoples!	3
For great is the Lord and greatly to be praised; He is terrible above all gods.	4
For all the gods of the peoples are idols; but the Lord made the heavens.	5
Praise and beauty are before Him; holiness and majesty are in His sanctuary.	6
Bring to the Lord, O families of the peoples, bring to the Lord glory and honor!	7

8   Bring to the Lord the glory due His name; bring offerings and come into His courts!
9   Worship the Lord in His holy court; let all the earth tremble before Him!
10   Say among the nations that the Lord is King!
For He has established the world so that it shall never be moved; He will judge the peoples with equity.
11   Let the heavens be glad, and let the earth rejoice; let the sea be moved, and all that fills it!
12   The field shall exult, and everything in it; then shall all the trees of the wood rejoice before the Face of the Lord;
13   for He comes, for He comes to judge the earth.
He will judge the world with righteousness and the peoples with His truth.

PSALM 96

1   The Lord reigns; let the earth rejoice; let the many coastlands be glad!
2   Clouds and darkness are round about Him; righteousness and justice are the foundation of His throne.
3   Fire shall go before Him and burn up His adversaries round about.
4   His lightnings appeared to the world; the earth saw and trembled.
5   The mountains melted like wax before the Face of the Lord, before the Face of the Lord of all the earth.

The heavens have proclaimed His righteousness, 6
and all the people have beheld His glory.
Let all worshipers of images be put to shame who 7
make their boast in their idols.
Bow down before Him, all His angels!
Zion heard and was glad, and the daughters of 8
Judah rejoiced because of Your judgments, O
Lord.
For You are Lord Most High over all the earth; 9
You are exalted far above all gods.
You that love the Lord, hate evil; the Lord 10
preserves the souls of His saints; He shall
deliver them from the hand of sinners.
Light dawns for the righteous and joy for the 11
upright in heart!
Rejoice in the Lord, O you righteous, and confess 12
the holiness of His name!

PSALM 97

Sing to the Lord a new song, for the Lord has 1
done marvelous things!
His right hand and His holy arm have wrought
salvation for Him.
The Lord has made known His salvation; He has 2
revealed His righteousness before the nations.
He has remembered His mercy to Jacob and His 3
truth to the house of Israel.
All the ends of the earth have seen the salvation of
our God!

4 Shout to God, all the earth; sing and exult and sing psalms!
5 Sing to the Lord with a lyre, with a lyre and the voice of a psalm!
6 With trumpets of metal and the sound of a trumpet of horn, make a joyful noise to the Lord before the king.
7 Let the sea be shaken and all its fullness, the world and those who dwell in it!
8 The rivers will clap their hands; the mountains will exult.
9 For He has come to judge the earth; He will judge the world in righteousness and the peoples with equity.

PSALM 98

1 The Lord reigns; let the peoples tremble! He sits enthroned upon the cherubim; let the earth quake!
2 The Lord is great in Zion; He is exalted over all the peoples.
3 Let them confess the greatness of Your name, for it is terrible and holy, and the king's honor is to love justice.
4 You have prepared equity; You have executed judgment and justice in Jacob.
5 Extol the Lord our God; worship at His footstool, for He is holy.

6 Moses and Aaron were among His priests; Samuel also was among those who called on His name; they cried to the Lord, and He answered them.
7 He spoke to them in the pillar of cloud; they kept His testimonies and the statutes that He gave them.
8 O Lord our God, You heard them; You were a forgiving God to them but an avenger of their wrongdoings.
9 Extol the Lord our God and worship at His holy mountain; for the Lord our God is holy!

PSALM 99

1 Make a joyful noise to the Lord, all the earth!
2 Serve the Lord with gladness! Come before His Face with exultation.
3 Know that the Lord is God! It is He who made us and not we ourselves; we are His people and the sheep of His pasture.
4 Enter into His gates with thanksgiving and His courts with praise; give thanks to Him, praise His name!
5 For the Lord is good; His mercy endures forever, and His truth from generation to generation.

PSALM 100

1 I will sing of mercy and of justice; to You, O Lord, I will sing a psalm.

2   I will have understanding of the perfect way;
   when will You come to me?
   I have walked with integrity of heart within my
   house;
3   I have not set before my eyes anything that is base;
   I hated the work of those who fall away.
4   The perverse of heart did not cleave to me; the
   evil man fled from me; I had no dealings with
   him.
5   Him who slanders his neighbor secretly I drove
   away;
   I did not eat with the man of haughty looks and
   greedy heart.
6   I looked with favor on the faithful in the land,
   that they may dwell with me.
   He who walks in the way that is blameless
   ministered to me.
7   No man who acts pridefully dwelt in my house;
   no man who utters lies continued in my presence.
8   Morning by morning I destroyed all the wicked in
   the land, cutting off all the evildoers from the
   city of the Lord.

✶ ✶ ✶

THE PHARISEE IN ME

If the Lord had not helped me, my soul would already have dwelt in Sheol.
PSALM 93:16

Whenever I read Bible stories about the Pharisees, I immediately conjure up images or instances involving people nowadays who, in my mind, have exhibited pharisaical behavior. I shake my head and wonder how it is that they don't realize it themselves. I clearly see the Pharisee in their behavior. But the real question is, do I see it in my own?

Let's be honest here: we're all hypocrites, at least some of the time, and some of the time is enough. We don't photograph our mistakes and post them on the internet next to a freshly picked bunch of wildflowers or the perfect latte for everyone to see and tell us how ridiculous they are. They're quietly folded and tucked deep down underneath our prouder moments and rarely see the light of day.

And in all honesty, we shouldn't shout them from the rooftops, where we might unknowingly encourage someone else to make the same mistakes. But there should be a cycle to our missteps—one that constantly leads back to repentance and forgiveness. We should never remember our sins and despair but should use them to remind us of just how far we still have to go. They should remind us to be watchful, knowing all too well that temptation can strike at any moment, and none of us is immune to its assault. Our shortcomings should humble us.

If we truly desire to overcome our pharisaical tendencies, we need to examine ourselves constantly and work hard to shed our former selves. Freeing ourselves from our old selves is hard work. If it's not, we're not doing it right.

The world teaches us a way of life that is very different from the way Christ has called us to live. Today's society has perhaps crossed over to the other end of the hypocritical spectrum by blurring the line between judgment and truth. The fact that someone says something is wrong doesn't make that person a Pharisee, nor does calling a sin by its name make someone judgmental. There is a definitive difference between right and wrong, and we need to make sure we understand it.

Truth should always be the due north of our moral compass, but it should be approached in a spirit of love rather than condemnation. The point of this whole Christian journey is to save our souls and to share the message of salvation through Christ. We can't do that by placing ourselves above others or by condoning sin.

So rather than waste our precious time making plans for everyone else's salvation, we should concentrate on removing the Pharisee in ourselves. Only then are we truly moving toward Christ.

Acquire the spirit of peace, and thousands around you will be saved.
ST. SERAPHIM OF SAROV[1]

---

1 Adi Da Samraj, ed., *The Spiritual Instructions of St. Seraphim of Sarov* (Lower Lake, CA: Dawn Horse Press, 2000).

JOURNALING PAGES

KATHISMA 14

PSALM 101

Hear my prayer, O Lord; let my cry come to You! 1
Do not turn Your Face from me in the day of my 2
distress!
Incline Your ear to me; hear me speedily in the
day when I call!
For my days have vanished like smoke, and my 3
bones have been parched like a stick.
I am blighted like grass, and my heart is withered, 4
for I have forgotten to eat my bread.
Because of my loud groaning, my bones cleave to 5
my flesh.
I have become like a pelican of the wilderness, 6
like an owl in a ruined house.
I have watched and have become like a lonely 7
sparrow on the housetop.
All the day my enemies taunt me; those who 8
praised me have sworn against me.
For I have eaten ashes like bread and mingle tears 9
with my drink because of Your indignation and 10
anger; for You have taken me up and thrown
me away.
My days have declined like a shadow; I wither 11
away like grass.
But You, O Lord, endure forever; Your memory is 12
from generation to generation.

13   You will arise and have mercy on Zion; it is time to have mercy on her; the time has come.
14   For Your servants hold her stones dear and have pity on her dust.
15   The nations will fear the name of the Lord, and all the kings of the earth Your glory.
16   For the Lord will build up Zion; He will appear
17   in His glory; He has regarded the prayer of the humble and has not despised their supplication.
18   Let this be recorded for a generation to come, so that a people yet uncreated shall praise the Lord:
19   for He has looked down from His holy height; from heaven the Lord looked at the earth
20   to hear the groans of the prisoners, to set free the sons of those who were slain,
21   to declare the name of the Lord in Zion, and in Jerusalem His praise,
22   when peoples gather together, and kings, to serve the Lord.
23   Man asked the Lord in the course of his strength, "Make me to know the shortness of my days."
24   Take me not away in the midst of my days: Your years endure throughout all generations!
25   You, O Lord, in the beginning laid the foundation of the earth, and the heavens are the work of Your hands.
26   They will perish, but You remain; and they will all grow old like a garment; like a cloak You will fold them up, and they will be changed.
27   But You are the same, and Your years will not fail.

The children of Your servants shall dwell securely; 28
their seed shall be led forever in the way of
righteousness.

PSALM 102

Bless the Lord, O my soul; and all that is within 1
me, bless His holy name!
Bless the Lord, O my soul, and forget not all His 2
benefits,
who forgives all your iniquity, who heals all your 3
diseases,
who redeems your life from the pit, who crowns 4
you with steadfast love and mercy,
who satisfies you with good as long as you live, so 5
that your youth is renewed like the eagle's.
The Lord works vindication and justice for all 6
who are oppressed.
He made known His ways to Moses, His acts to 7
the people of Israel.
The Lord is compassionate and merciful, long- 8
suffering and of great goodness.
He will not always chide, nor will He keep His 9
anger forever.
He does not deal with us according to our sins nor 10
requite us according to our iniquities.
For as the heavens are high above the earth, so 11
great is His steadfast love toward those who fear
Him;
as far as the east is from the west, so far does He 12
remove our transgressions from us.

13 As a father pities his children, so the Lord pities those who fear Him.
14 For He knows our frame; He remembers that we are dust.
15 As for man, his days are like grass; he flourishes like a flower of the field;
16 for the wind passes over it, and it is gone, and its place knows it no more.
17 But the steadfast love of the Lord is from everlasting to everlasting upon those who fear Him, and His righteousness to children's children,
18 to those who keep His covenant and remember to do His commandments.
19 The Lord has established His throne in the heavens, and His kingdom rules over all.
20 Bless the Lord, O you His angels, you mighty ones who do His word, hearkening to the voice of His word!
21 Bless the Lord, all His hosts, His ministers that do His will!
22 Bless the Lord, all His works, in all places of His dominion.
Bless the Lord, O my soul! In all places of His dominion. Bless the Lord, O my soul!

PSALM 103

1 Bless the Lord, O my soul. O Lord, my God, You are very great.
2 You are clothed with honor and majesty, who cover Yourself with light as with a garment;

who have stretched out the heavens like a tent.

Who have laid the beams of Your chambers on the waters,   3

who make the clouds Your chariot, who ride on the wings of the wind.

Who make Your angels spirits and Your ministers a fiery flame.   4

You set the earth on its foundations so that it should never be shaken.   5

You covered it with the deep as with a garment; the waters stood above the mountains.   6

At Your rebuke they fled; at the sound of Your thunder they took to flight.   7

The mountains rose; the valleys sank down to the place which You appointed for them.   8

You set a boundary which they should not pass, so that they might not again cover the earth.   9

You make springs gush forth in the valleys; they flow between the hills.   10

They give drink to every beast of the field; the wild asses quench their thirst.   11

By them the birds of the air have their habitation; they sing among the branches.   12

From Your lofty abode You water the mountains; the earth is satisfied with the fruit of Your work.   13

You caused the grass to grow for the cattle, fodder for the animals that serve man.   14

That He may bring forth food from the earth, and wine to gladden the heart of man,   15

oil to make his face shine, and bread to strengthen man's heart.

16 The trees of the Lord are watered abundantly, the cedars of Lebanon which He planted.
17 In them the birds build their nests; the stork has her home in the fir trees.
18 The high mountains are for the wild goats; the rocks are a refuge for the badgers.
19 You have made the moon to mark the seasons. The sun knows its time for setting.
20 You make darkness, and it is night, when all the beasts of the forest creep forth.
21 The young lions roar for their prey, seeking their food from God.
22 When the sun rises, they get them away and lie down in their dens.
23 Man goes forth to his work and to his labor until the evening.
24 O Lord, how manifold are Your works. In wisdom have You made them all. The earth is full of Your creatures.
25 Yonder is the sea, great and wide, which teems with things innumerable, living things both small and great.
26 There go the ships, and Leviathan which You formed to sport in it.
27 These all look to You, to give them their food in due season.
28 When You give to them, they gather it up; when You open Your hand, they are filled with good things.
29 When You hide Your Face, they are dismayed; when You take away their spirit, they die and return to their dust.

When You send forth Your Spirit, they are created, and You renew the face of the earth. 30

May the glory of the Lord endure forever. May the Lord rejoice in His works. 31

Who looks on the earth and it trembles; who touches the mountains and they smoke. 32

I will sing to the Lord as long as I live; I will sing praises to my God while I have being. 33

May my meditation be pleasing to Him, for I rejoice in the Lord. 34

Let sinners be consumed from the earth, and let the wicked be no more. 35

Bless the Lord, O my soul. Praise the Lord!

PSALM 104

O give thanks to the Lord, call on His name; make known His deeds among the peoples! 1

Sing to Him, sing praises to Him; tell of all His wonderful works! 2

Glory in His holy name; let the hearts of those who seek the Lord rejoice! 3

Seek the Lord and He will give You strength; seek His Face continually. 4

Remember the wonderful works that He has done, His miracles, and the judgments He uttered, 5

O offspring of Abraham His servant, sons of Jacob, His chosen ones! 6

He is the Lord our God; His judgments are in all the earth. 7

8 He is mindful of His covenant forever, of the word that He commanded, for a thousand generations,
9 the covenant which He made with Abraham,
10 His sworn promise to Isaac, which He confirmed to Jacob as a statute, to Israel as an everlasting covenant, saying,
11 "To you I will give the land of Canaan as your portion for an inheritance."
12 When they were few in number, of little account and foreigners in the land,
13 wandering from nation to nation, from one kingdom to another people,
14 He allowed no one to oppress them; He rebuked kings on their account, saying,
15 "Touch not those whom I have anointed; do my prophets no harm!"
16 He summoned a famine on the land and broke every staff of bread.
17 He sent a man ahead of them; Joseph was sold as a slave.
18 His feet were hurt with fetters; his neck was put in a collar of iron
19 until His word came to pass; the word of the Lord tested him like fire.
20 The king sent and released him; the ruler of the peoples set him free;
21 he made him lord of his house and ruler of all his possessions,
22 to instruct his princes at his pleasure and to teach his elders wisdom.

Then Israel came to Egypt; Jacob sojourned in the land of Ham.	23
And the Lord made His people very fruitful and made them stronger than their foes.	24
He turned their hearts to hate His people, to deal craftily with His servants.	25
He sent Moses His servant and Aaron whom He had chosen.	26
They wrought His signs among them and miracles in the land of Ham.	27
He sent darkness and made the land dark; yet they rebelled against His words.	28
He turned their waters into blood and caused their fish to die.	29
Their land swarmed with frogs, even in the chambers of the kings;	30
He spoke, and there came swarms of flies and gnats throughout their country.	31
He gave them hail for rain and lightning that flashed through their land.	32
He smote their vines and fig trees and shattered the trees of their country.	33
He spoke and the locusts came, and young locusts without number,	34
which devoured all the vegetation in their land and ate up the fruit of their ground.	35
He smote all the firstborn in their land, the first fruits of all their labor.	36
Then He led them forth with silver and gold, and there was not a feeble one among their tribes.	37
Egypt was glad when they departed, for dread of them had fallen upon it.	38

39 He spread a cloud as a covering for them and fire to give light by night.
40 They asked, and the quail came, and He satisfied them with the bread of heaven.
41 He opened the rock, and water gushed forth; it flowed through the desert like a river.
42 For He remembered His holy word to Abraham His servant.
43 So He led forth His people with joy, His chosen ones with exultation.
44 And He gave them the lands of the nations; and they took possession of the fruit of the people's toil,
45 to the end that they should keep His statutes, and diligently seek His laws.

✠ ✠ ✠

MY BEAUTIFUL MESS

You have made the moon to mark the seasons.
The sun knows its time for setting.
PSALM 103:18

I used to pride myself on my ability to multitask and felt good about being able to effectively juggle so many different tasks at once. That is, until my arms grew tired and I just didn't want to juggle anymore. All of a sudden I felt I was losing a part of myself. I wasn't doing some of the things I really loved to do and had begun missing out on the very things I said I never would. Those quiet mornings on the front porch swing with my husband were becoming hurried. Climbing monkey bars with my kids at the park turned into watching them climb while I answered emails and other messages. My body still went through some of the motions, but the memories seemed further away somehow, as if I were watching it all from the wrong end of a looking glass.

All my life, I've been the kind of person who savored the little things, but I began to realize I was so busy being "productive" that some of those precious moments were slipping through my fingers, and that terrified me. My ability to multitask began to hold me back from making real life happen.

On our way home from the park one day, I listened as my kids laughed and talked about a game they were playing. Normally, I would have known exactly what they were talking about because I was usually out there playing it with them, but this time I had no idea. At that moment, I knew I had to force myself to slow down and reprioritize my life.

That night, when everyone was in bed, I took out my journal and made a list of my priorities. It looked something like this:

1. Spiritual life (prayer, reading, serving)
2. Family (school, quality time)
3. Work (home business, writing, blogging)
4. Leisure (knitting, reading, gardening, painting, etc.)

As I looked at my list, I realized that the items on my leisure list sort of came in seasons. Gardening was more of a spring and summer hobby for me, and I tend to knit most in the fall. To everything there is a season (Ecc. 3:11). Maybe all my life needed was a little reorganizing. I made a few more notes on how I could be more present in the present again and promised to be careful not to let anything derail me from my first three priorities: faith, family, and our livelihood.

Next, I made a list of my distractions. It was a pretty short list that looked exactly like this:

1. Cell phone

Sound familiar? It was quite literally the only thing I could think of that was a real distraction. I decided that the only time my phone would come out of my bag while making memories was to capture them. No sharing photos on Instagram or texting them to family until later. This was really hard at first, and I was surprised by how often I reached for my phone; but I kept reminding myself that I'd never get that moment again. The right here and now, my children sliding down that slide or telling me that story or snuggling on my lap, will never happen just like this again. Ever.

For us as busy women, it's impossible not to multitask to some extent, but as Orthodox women, we have to remember the healing power of being still. It's in those moments of stillness that the fog is wiped from our glasses and we see life for what it truly is—a beautiful mess. The days are long sometimes, but the years are much too short. I, for one, want to stop and breathe in every crazy-beautiful-messy moment I'm blessed to see.

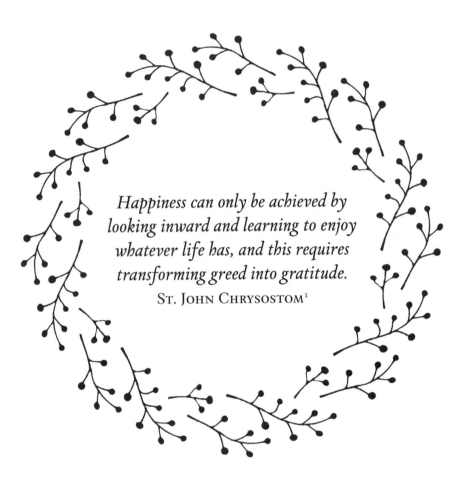

Happiness can only be achieved by looking inward and learning to enjoy whatever life has, and this requires transforming greed into gratitude.
ST. JOHN CHRYSOSTOM[1]

---

1 St. John Chrysostom, *On Wealth and Poverty*.

JOURNALING PAGES

KATHISMA 15

PSALM 105

1. O give thanks to the Lord, for He is good; for His mercy endures forever.
2. Who shall utter the mighty doings of the Lord or make all His praises to be heard?
3. Blessed are those who keep judgment and do righteousness at all times!
4. Remember us, O Lord, with the favor you show to Your people; visit us with Your salvation,
5. that we may see the prosperity of Your chosen ones; that we may rejoice in the gladness of Your nation; that we may glory with Your heritage.
6. We have sinned with our fathers; we have transgressed; we have done unrighteously.
7. Our fathers, when they were in Egypt, did not understand Your wonders; they did not remember the abundance of Your mercy but provoked You as they went up by the Red Sea.
8. Yet He saved them for His name's sake, that He might make known His mighty power.
9. He rebuked the Red Sea, and it became dry; so He led them through the deep as through a desert.
10. He saved them from the hand of those who hated them and redeemed them from the hand of the enemy.

11   The waters covered their oppressors; not one of them was left.
12   Then they believed His words and celebrated His praise.
13   But they made haste to forget His works; they did not wait to know His counsel.
14   They had a wanton craving in the wilderness and tempted God in the waterless land;
15   He gave them what they asked and sent fullness into their souls.
16   They provoked Moses in the camp, and Aaron, the holy one of the Lord;
17   the earth opened and swallowed up Dathan and covered the company of Abiram.
18   A fire was kindled in their midst; a flame burned up the sinners.
19   They made a calf in Horeb and worshiped the graven image;
20   they exchanged their Glory for the likeness of a calf that eats grass.
21   They forgot God, who saved them, who had done great deeds in Egypt,
22   wondrous works in the land of Ham and terrible things by the Red Sea.
23   Therefore, He said, He would have destroyed them, had not Moses, His chosen one, stood in the breach before Him,
     to turn away the fierceness of His wrath so that He should not destroy them.
24   But they despised the pleasant land and did not believe His word.

They murmured in their tents and did not listen	25
to the voice of the Lord.	
Therefore He raised His hand against them to cast	26
them down in the wilderness,	
and to cast down their seed among the nations,	27
and to scatter them in the lands.	
They were attached also to the Baal of Peor and	28
ate the sacrifices of the dead;	
and they provoked the Lord with their doings, and	29
destruction was multiplied among them.	
Then Phineas stood up and obtained forgiveness,	30
and the plague was stayed.	
And that was reckoned to him as righteousness	31
from generation to generation forever.	
They provoked Him also at the waters of Strife,	32
and Moses was hurt on their account;	
for they provoked his spirit, and he spoke words	33
that were rash.	
They did not destroy the peoples, as the Lord	34
commanded them, but they mingled with the	35
nations and learned to do as they did.	
They served their graven images, which became a	36
snare to them.	
They sacrificed their sons and their daughters to	37
the demons;	
they poured out innocent blood, the blood of their	38
sons and daughters, whom they sacrificed to the	
idols of Canaan;	
the land was polluted with blood and became	39
unclean by their acts; they played the harlot in	
their doings.	

40 Therefore the anger of the Lord was kindled against His people, and He abhorred His heritage;
41 He gave them into the hands of the nations, and those who hated them ruled over them.
42 Their enemies oppressed them, and they were brought into subjection under their hands.
43 Many times He delivered them, but they provoked Him by their counsel and were brought low through their iniquities.
44 Nevertheless, the Lord regarded their distress when He heard their petition.
45 He remembered His covenant and relented according to the abundance of His mercy.
46 He caused them to be pitied in the sight of all those who carried them away captive.
47 Save us, O Lord our God, and gather us from among the nations,
that we may confess Your holy name and glory in praising You.
48 Blessed be the Lord, the God of Israel, from everlasting to everlasting!
And all the people shall say, "Amen! Amen!"

PSALM 106

1 O give thanks to the Lord, for He is good; for His mercy endures forever!
2 Let the redeemed of the Lord say so, whom He has redeemed from the hand of the enemy

and gathered in from the lands, from the east and from the west, from the north and from the south.	3
They wandered in the desert, in a waterless land, without finding the city they were to dwell in;	4
hungry and thirsty, their soul fainted within them.	5
Then they cried to the Lord in their trouble, and He delivered them from their distresses;	6
He led them to a straight way, that they might reach the city they were to dwell in.	7
Let them confess the Lord for His mercies and His wonderful works to the sons of men;	8
for He satisfies the thirsty, and the hungry He fills with good things.	9
They were sitting in darkness and the shadow of death, chained in poverty and in irons,	10
because they had rebelled against the words of God and had despised the counsel of the Most High.	11
So their hearts were bowed down with labors; they were weak, and there was no helper.	12
Then they cried to the Lord in their trouble, and He delivered them from their distresses;	13
He brought them out of darkness and the shadow of death and broke their bonds asunder.	14
Let them confess the Lord for His mercies and His wonderful works to the sons of men!	15
For He shattered the doors of bronze and crushed the bars of iron.	16
He helped them out of their sinful way, for they were brought low because of their iniquities;	17

18 their soul loathed all food, and they drew near to the gates of death.
19 Then they cried to the Lord in their trouble, and He delivered them from their distresses;
20 He sent forth His Word and healed them, and delivered them from their corruption.
21 Let them confess the Lord for His mercies and His wonderful works to the sons of men!
22 And let them offer to Him the sacrifice of praise and tell of His deeds with exultation!
23 Those who go down to the sea in ships, doing business on many waters,
24 have seen the deeds of the Lord and His wondrous works in the deep.
25 He spoke, and the stormy wind arose, and its waves were lifted up.
26 They mounted up to the heavens, they went down to the depths; their souls melted away because of their troubles;
27 they reeled and staggered like drunken men, and all their wisdom was swallowed up.
28 Then they cried to the Lord in their trouble, and He delivered them from their distress;
29 and He commanded the storm, and it was calmed to a gentle breeze, and its waves were stilled.
30 Then they were glad because they had quiet, and He guided them to their desired haven.
31 Let them confess the Lord for His mercies and His wonderful works to the sons of men!
32 Let them extol Him in the congregation of the people and praise Him in the council of the elders.

For He turned rivers into a desert, springs of water into thirsty ground, and a fruitful land into a salty waste because of the wickedness of its inhabitants.	33 34

He turned the desert into pools of water, parched land into springs of water. 35

And there He settled the hungry, and they established the city they were to dwell in. 36

They sowed fields, and planted vineyards, and gathered fruits of all sorts. 37

He blessed them, and they multiplied greatly; and He did not let their flocks decrease. 38

But afterward they were diminished and brought low through the afflictions of tribulation and suffering. 39

Contempt was poured upon their princes, and He made them wander in a desert and trackless waste; 40

but He helped the poor out of poverty and made their families like a flock. 41

The upright shall see and be glad, and all wickedness shall stop its mouth. 42

Who is wise to give heed to these things and understand the mercy of the Lord? 43

PSALM 107

My heart, O God, is ready, my heart is ready. 1
   I will sing, yes, I will sing psalms!
Awake, O my soul! Awake, O harp and lyre! 2
   I will awake the dawn!

3   I will confess You, O Lord, among the peoples;
      I will sing praises to You among the nations.
4   For Your mercy is higher than the heavens, and
      Your truth reaches to the clouds.
5   Be exalted, O God, above the heavens, and Your
      glory over all the earth!
6   That Your beloved may be delivered, save by Your
      right hand and hear me!
7   God has spoken in His sanctuary: "I will be
      exalted and will divide up Shechem and portion
      out the valley of Succoth.
8   Gilead is Mine and Manasseh is Mine; Ephraim is
      the protection of My head; Judah is My king.
9   Moab is My washbasin; upon Edom I will cast My
      shoe; the Philistines are subjected to Me."
10 Who will bring me to the fortified city? Who will
      lead me to Edom?
11 Will not You, O God, although You have rejected
      us? Will not You, O God, go forth with our
      armies?
12 Oh, grant us help in times of tribulation, for vain
      is the help of man!
13 With God we shall do valiantly; it is He who will
      bring our foes down to nothing.

PSALM 108

1   O God, do not pass over my praise in silence!
2   For the mouth of the wicked and the mouth of
      the deceitful are opened against me, speaking
      against me with lying tongues.

They beset me with words of hate and attack me without cause.	3
In return for my love, they falsely accused me, but I continued to pray for them.	4
They rewarded me evil for good and hatred for my love.	5
And they say, "Appoint a sinner against him; let the Accuser stand at his right hand.	6
When he is tried, let him come forth condemned; let his prayer be counted as sin.	7
May his days be few; may another seize his high office.	8
May his children be fatherless and his wife a widow.	9
May his sons wander without a dwelling and beg; may they be driven out of the ruins they inhabit.	10
May the creditor seize all that he has; may strangers plunder the fruit of his toil.	11
Let him have no helper, nor anyone to pity his fatherless children.	12
May his children be utterly destroyed; may his name be blotted out in one generation.	13
May the iniquity of his fathers be remembered before the Lord, and let not the sin of his mother be blotted out; let them be before the Lord continually.	14
And may their memory be cut off from the earth.	15
For he did not remember to show mercy but persecuted the poor and needy and the brokenhearted to their death.	16

17 He loved to curse; let curses come on him!
He did not like blessing; may it be far from him!
18 He clothed himself with cursing as his coat; may it soak into his body like water, like oil into his bones.
19 May it be like a garment which he wraps round him, like a belt with which he continually girds himself."
20 This is the work of those who falsely accuse me before the Lord, of those who speak evil against my soul.
21 But You, O Lord, deal mercifully with me for Your name's sake, for Your mercy is good.
22 Deliver me, for I am poor and needy, and my heart is stricken within me.
23 I am gone, like a shadow at evening; I am shaken off like a locust.
24 My knees are weak through fasting; my body has become gaunt for lack of oil.
25 I am a reproach to them; when they see me, they wag their heads.
26 Help me, O Lord my God! Save me according to Your mercy,
27 that they may know that this is Your hand; that You, O Lord, have done it!
28 Let them curse, but You shall bless.
Let my assailants be put to shame; let Your servant be glad!
29 Let those who falsely accuse me be clothed with dishonor; may they be wrapped in their own shame as in a mantle!

With a loud voice, I will confess the Lord; I will praise Him in the midst of the throng. 30

For He stands at the right hand of the poor man to save my soul from those who persecute me. 31

☩ ☩ ☩

A HOMEMAKER'S PRAYER

*O give thanks to the Lord, for He is good;
for His mercy endures forever.*
PSALM 105:1

Sometimes, out of nowhere, I get overcome with the desire to pray. I feel a tugging inside my heart, and I long to be closer to God. I'll be driving home from someplace and think, "As soon as I get home, I'm going straight to the prayer corner to pray!" But by the time I get home, even if it's a short distance, I'm immediately distracted by all the things demanding my attention. Laundry needs to be done, dinner needs to be prepped, counters need to be decluttered, kids need help with homework. The list seems endless. That spark of zeal is snuffed out before it has a chance to become a flame, and I'm left feeling overwhelmed and discouraged. That's when I remind myself of the goodness of God. I remind myself that He will accept my best efforts despite how meager they might be.

God knows what we need and will provide it. Practicing the art of prayer does not need to consist of long services, as nice as that would be sometimes. I don't need to wait until I get home to pray; I can unroll the prayer rope from my wrist and begin saying the Jesus Prayer as I drive. After all, isn't that why I wear it?

This is only one of the reasons I am so grateful to have an experienced spiritual father. His advice is invaluable, especially when it comes to practicing prayer. A spiritual father will guide you. He will give you a prayer rule according to your individual needs, and that prayer rule will help you grow not only in prayer but also in obedience. Sometimes when I'm feeling zealous I'll want to read an extra service, like an Akathist or

Paraklesis, but then when it's time for my prayer rule in the evening, I'll feel tired and not want to do it. My spiritual father then reminds me that while it's great to do extra services, we need to make sure we're doing our prayer rule first. Obedience is what will help us grow, not only in prayer but in all spiritual things.

Every member of my family can attest to the power of obedience, not because we're good at it, but because when we're not so good at it, each one of us feels it. When we're keeping our prayer rules—services, prostrations, Jesus Prayer, and Scripture reading—life happens smoothly. When we're not, it doesn't. It's not that outside circumstances necessarily change. What changes is our ability to handle those circumstances. When we pray, we find in ourselves a strength that isn't our own. It's easy not to notice that strength when you're in the thick of things, but when you look back, you marvel at how on earth you ever made it through in one piece. *That* is what God does for us through prayer.

While I for one certainly don't have the strength or discipline of the saints, or even of a pious layperson for that matter, I will still fight the devil, who works tirelessly to discourage me and tries to make me grumble about my blessings. I will scrub those pots and pans with all my might while repeating the Jesus Prayer. As I prepare dinner for my family, I will give thanks to God for blessing me with both a family to feed and food to prepare for them. I will struggle to turn my sighs into prayers, my housework into quiet hopes of salvation.

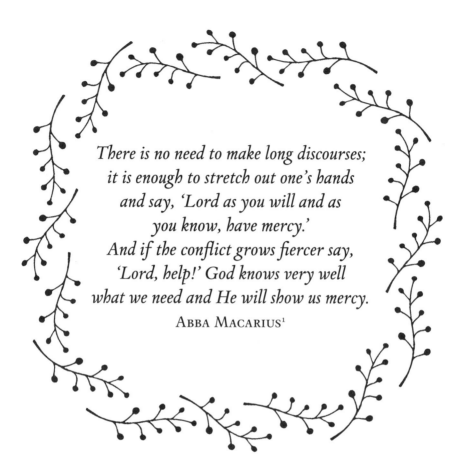

*There is no need to make long discourses;
it is enough to stretch out one's hands
and say, 'Lord as you will and as
you know, have mercy.'
And if the conflict grows fiercer say,
'Lord, help!' God knows very well
what we need and He will show us mercy.*

ABBA MACARIUS[1]

---

[1] Benedicta Ward, trans., *The Sayings of the Desert Fathers: The Alphabetical Collection* (Collegeville, MN: Liturgical Press, 1984).

JOURNALING PAGES

KATHISMA 16

PSALM 109

1. The Lord said to my Lord, "Sit at My right hand till I make Your enemies Your footstool."
2. The Lord sends forth from Zion Your mighty scepter. Rule in the midst of Your foes!
3. With You is dominion on the day of Your birth, in the radiance of holiness; out of the womb before the morning star have I begotten You.
4. The Lord has sworn and will not change His mind: You are a priest forever after the order of Melchizedek!
5. The Lord at Your right hand has shattered kings in the day of His wrath.
6. He will judge the nations, filling them with corpses; He will crush the heads of many on the earth.
7. He will drink from the brook by the way; therefore He will lift up his head.

PSALM 110

1. I will confess You, O Lord, with my whole heart in the company of the upright, in the congregation; great are the works of the Lord.
2. They are studied by all who have pleasure in them.

3   His work is glory and beauty, and His righteousness endures forever.
4   He has caused His wonderful works to be remembered; the Lord is compassionate and merciful.
5   He has provided food for those who fear Him; He will always remember His covenant.
6   He has declared to His people the power of His works, to give them the heritage of the peoples.
7   The works of His hands are truth and judgment; all His precepts are trustworthy;
8   they are established forever and ever, performed in truth and uprightness.
9   The Lord has sent redemption to His people; He has commanded His covenant forever. Holy and terrible is His name!
10 The fear of the Lord is the beginning of wisdom; a good understanding have all those who practice it.
    His praise endures forever and ever!

PSALM 111

1   Blessed is the man who fears the Lord, who greatly delights in His commandments!
2   His descendants will be mighty on the earth; the generation of the upright shall be blessed!
3   Glory and wealth are in his house, and his righteousness endures forever.
4   Light rises in the darkness for the upright; the Lord is merciful, compassionate, and righteous.

It is well with the man who deals mercifully and 5
lends, who conducts his affairs with justice; for
he will never be moved.
The righteous will be remembered forever; he is 6
not afraid of evil tidings.
His heart is firm, trusting in the Lord; his heart 7
is steady; he will not be afraid until he sees his 8
enemies routed.
He has scattered freely abroad; he has given to the 9
poor; his righteousness endures forever; his
horn will be exalted in glory.
The sinner will see it and be angry; he will gnash 10
his teeth and wither away; the desire of the
sinner will perish.

PSALM 112

Praise the Lord, O you servants of the Lord; 1
praise the name of the Lord!
Blessed be the name of the Lord, henceforth and 2
forevermore.
From the rising of the sun to its setting, let the 3
name of the Lord be praised!
The Lord is exalted above all nations and His 4
glory above the heavens!
Who is like the Lord our God, who dwells on 5
high, who looks down upon the heavens and 6
the earth?
He raises the poor from the dust and lifts the 7
needy from the dunghill,

8 to set him with princes, with the princes of His people.
9 He gives the barren woman a home, making her the joyous mother of children.

PSALM 113

1 When Israel went forth from Egypt, the house of Jacob from a people of strange language,
2 Judah became his sanctuary, Israel his dominion.
3 The sea looked and fled; Jordan was driven back.
4 The mountains skipped like rams, the hills like lambs.
5 What ails you, O sea, that you flee? O Jordan, that you turn back?
6 How is it, O mountains, that you skipped like rams and you hills, like lambs?
7 The earth trembled before the Face of the Lord, before the Face of the God of Jacob,
8 Who turned the rock into pools of water, the flint into springs of water.
9 Not to us, O Lord, not to us, but to Your name give glory, for the sake of Your mercy and Your truth,
10 lest the nations should say, "Where is their God?"
11 Our God is in heaven and on earth; He does whatever He pleases.
12 The idols of the nations are silver and gold, the works of men's hands.
13 They have mouths, but do not speak; eyes, but do not see.

14 They have ears, but do not hear; noses, but do not smell.
15 They have hands, but do not feel; feet, but do not walk; and they do not make a sound in their throat.
16 Let those who make them be like them, and all who trust in them.
17 The house of Israel trusts in the Lord; He is their helper and defender.
18 The house of Aaron trusts in the Lord; He is their helper and defender.
19 Those who fear the Lord trust in the Lord; He is their helper and defender.
20 The Lord has been mindful of us; He has blessed us;
He has blessed the house of Israel; He has blessed the house of Aaron;
21 He has blessed those who fear the Lord, both small and great.
22 May the Lord give you increase, you and your children!
23 May you be blessed by the Lord, who made heaven and earth!
24 The heavens are the Lord's heavens, but the earth He has given to the sons of men.
25 The dead will not praise the Lord, nor any that go down into Sheol.
26 But we who live will bless the Lord from this time forth and forevermore.

PSALM 114

1 I love the Lord because He has heard the voice of my supplication.
2 Because He inclined His ear to me, therefore I will call on Him as long as I live.
3 The snares of death encompassed me; the pangs of Sheol laid hold on me;
4 I suffered distress and anguish; then I called upon the name of the Lord: "O Lord, deliver my soul!"
5 Gracious and righteous is the Lord, and our God is merciful.
6 The Lord preserves the simple; when I was brought low, He saved me.
7 Return, O my soul, to your rest; for the Lord has dealt bountifully with you.
8 For He has delivered my soul from death, my eyes from tears, my feet from stumbling;
9 therefore, I desire to please the Lord in the land of the living.

PSALM 115

1 I believed, therefore I spoke; but I was greatly humiliated.
2 I said in my anger, "Every man is a liar."
3 What shall I render to the Lord for all that He has given me?

I will take up the cup of salvation and call on the 4
   name of the Lord.
I will pay my vows to the Lord in the presence of
   all His people.
Precious in the sight of the Lord is the death of 5
   His saints.
O Lord, I am Your servant; I am Your servant and 6
   the son of Your handmaid; You have broken my
   bonds.
I will offer You the sacrifice of praise and call 7
   upon the name of the Lord.
I will pay my vows to the Lord in the presence of 8
   all His people,
in the courts of the house of the Lord, in your 9
   midst, O Jerusalem! Praise the Lord!

PSALM 116

Praise the Lord, all nations! Praise Him, all 1
   peoples!
For His mercy is confirmed on us; and the truth of 2
   the Lord endures forever. Praise the Lord!

PSALM 117

O give thanks to the Lord, for He is good, 1
   for His mercy endures forever!
Let the house of Israel say, "He is good, 2
   for His mercy endures forever!"
Let the house of Aaron say, "He is good, 3
   for His mercy endures forever!"

4   Let all who fear the Lord say, "He is good,
      for His mercy endures forever!"
5   Out of my distress I called on the Lord; the Lord
      answered me and set me free.
6   The Lord is my helper; I will not fear what man
      can do to me.
7   The Lord is my helper; I shall look in triumph
      over my enemies.
8   It is better to trust in the Lord than to trust in
9   man; it is better to hope in the Lord than to
      hope in princes.
10   All nations surrounded me; but in the name of the
      Lord I withstood them.
11   They surrounded me, surrounded me on every
      side; but in the name of the Lord I withstood
      them.
12   They surrounded me like bees, they blazed like
      a fire of thorns; but in the name of the Lord I
      withstood them.
13   I was pushed hard so that I was falling, but the
      Lord helped me.
14   The Lord is my strength and my song; He has
      become my salvation.
15   The voice of exultation and salvation is in the
      tents of the righteous:
16   "The right hand of the Lord has worked wonders!
      The right hand of the Lord has exalted me; the
      right hand of the Lord has worked wonders!"
17   I shall not die, but I shall live and recount the
      deeds of the Lord.
18   The Lord has chastened me sorely, but He has not
      given me over to death.

19 Open to me the gates of righteousness; I will enter through them and confess the Lord.
20 This is the gate of the Lord; the righteous shall enter through it.
21 I will thank You, for You have answered me and have become my salvation.
22 The stone which the builders rejected has become
23 the head of the corner. This is the Lord's doing, and it is marvelous in our eyes.
24 This is the day which the Lord has made! Let us rejoice and be glad in it!
25 Save us now, O Lord! O Lord, lead us to victory!
26 Blessed is he that comes in the name of the Lord! We bless you from the house of the Lord! God is the Lord and has revealed Himself to us!
27 Celebrate the feast with many branches, up to the horns of the altar.
28 You are my God, and I will confess You; You are my God, and I will extol You.
I will praise You, for You have heard me and have become my salvation.
29 O give thanks to the Lord, for He is good, for His mercy endures forever!

✠ ✠ ✠

THE WORLD NEEDS MORE LOVE
(LETTERS)

Not to us, O Lord, not to us, but to Your name give glory.
PSALM 113:8

Love is a word that is thrown around like confetti in today's society. Yet it feels as if people are more disconnected and intolerant than ever. Everyone talks about love, yet few actually show it.

Several years ago, I ran across a project called "If You Find This Letter." The basic concept is to write letters of encouragement anonymously and leave them in random places for strangers to find. The idea captivated me for several reasons. First, I loved the idea of writing letters anonymously. With plaques and shout-outs for every little thing we do these days, I loved the idea that there was no praise or thanks involved. I also really loved the idea of leaving a handwritten letter full of encouraging words for someone I'd never meet.

I decided instead of only writing random words, I'd include a scripture verse or quotation that expressed God's perfect love. What better love is there than His? It felt like the perfect way to spread His message without having to get into awkward conversations and having some of that previously mentioned confetti shoved down my throat. If someone didn't like what I had to say in my letter, they could simply throw it away. But what if they took the words to heart, and a seed was planted? What if someone found encouragement and felt the love of God? *What if?*

That afternoon, I picked up several packs of notecards and started writing. I had no plan for what I would say; I just started writing. Somehow when the ink started to flow, the words began to pour out. I pulled out my notebook and copied some of my favorite quotations and scripture verses along with things I thought someone might need to hear. There's no rhyme or reason to what I write, other than it being from the heart.

My goal is for each and every letter to make someone feel loved. Sometimes, when you have a family and friends who love you, you take it for granted and assume everyone experiences that same love. But that's not the case. There are people in the world who have no one cheering them on or making them feel cherished. And they should.

I never sign my name, just "Sincerely, Someone who believes in you" or "From someone who cares." Then I seal the letter, and on the front of the envelope I write, "If you find this letter . . . It's for you" with the hashtag #moreloveletters. It's a lot of fun searching that hashtag and seeing not only letters people are writing but the ones people have found.

My little love letters have been scattered across the country—from rooftop cafes in New York City to park benches in the Grand Canyon and even on a seat in the Grand Ole Opry. The people I'm with usually don't even know I'm doing it—I just linger a moment and quietly set an envelope down before moseying on my way.

The point is to spread the love far and wide. In a world full of uncertainties, one thing is for sure: The world really does need more love (letters).

The person who loves God cannot help loving every man as himself.
St. Maximos the Confessor[1]

---

[1] St. Maximos the Confessor, "Four Hundred Texts on Love" 1.13, in *The Philokalia: The Complete Text,* Vol. 2 (New York: Farrar, Strauss & Giroux, 1982).

JOURNALING PAGES

KATHISMA 17

PSALM 118

1. Blessed are those whose way is blameless, who walk in the law of the Lord.
2. Blessed are those who keep His testimonies, who seek Him with their whole heart.
3. For those who work wickedness have not walked in His ways.
4. You have commanded Your precepts to be kept diligently.
5. Oh, that my ways may be steadfast in keeping Your statutes!
6. Then I shall not be put to shame, having my eyes fixed on all Your commandments.
7. I will praise You with an upright heart when I learn Your righteous ordinances.
8. I will observe Your statutes; O forsake me not utterly.
9. How can a young man keep his way pure? By guarding it according to Your word.
10. With my whole heart I seek You; let me not wander from Your commandments.
11. I have hidden Your word in my heart, that I might not sin against You.
12. Blessed are You, O Lord! Teach me Your statutes!
13. With my lips I declare all the ordinances of Your mouth.

14 In the way of Your testimonies I delight, as much as in all riches.
15 I will meditate on Your precepts and fix my eyes on Your ways.
16 I will delight in Your statutes; I will not forget Your word.
17 Deal bountifully with Your servant; give me life, and I shall keep Your word.
18 Open my eyes, that I may behold wondrous things out of Your law.
19 I am only a sojourner on earth; hide not Your commandments from me.
20 My soul is consumed with longing for Your ordinances at all times.
21 You have rebuked the proud, and cursed are those who wander from Your commandments.
22 Take away from me their scorn and contempt, for I have kept Your testimonies.
23 Even though princes sit plotting against me, Your servant will meditate on Your statutes.
24 Your testimonies are my delight; they are my counselors.
25 My soul cleaves to the dust; give me life according to Your word.
26 When I told of my ways, You answered me; teach me Your statutes!
27 Make me understand the way of Your precepts, and I will meditate on Your wondrous works.
28 My soul melts away for sorrow; strengthen me according to Your word.
29 Put false ways far from me and graciously teach me Your law.

30 I have chosen the way of truth; I have not forgotten Your ordinances.
31 I cleave to Your testimonies, O Lord; let me not be put to shame.
32 I will run in the way of Your commandments when You have enlarged my heart.
33 Teach me, O Lord, the way of Your statutes, and I will keep it to the end.
34 Give me understanding, that I may keep Your law and observe it with my whole heart.
35 Lead me in the path of Your commandments, for I delight in it.
36 Incline my heart to Your testimonies and not to gain.
37 Turn my eyes from looking at vanities, and give me life in Your ways.
38 Establish Your promise in Your servant, that I may fear You.
39 Take away the reproach which I dread; for Your ordinances are good.
40 Behold, I long for Your precepts; in Your righteousness give me life.
41 Let Your mercy come to me, O Lord, and your salvation, according to Your word.
42 So shall I give an answer to those who taunt me, for I trust in Your word.
43 And take not the word of truth utterly out of my mouth, for my hope is in Your ordinances.
44 I will keep Your law continually forever and ever.
45 And I shall walk at liberty, for I have sought Your precepts.

46 I also spoke of Your testimonies before kings and was not ashamed.
47 For I find my delight in Your commandments, which I love exceedingly.
48 I lift up my hands to Your commandments, which I love, and I will meditate on Your statutes.
49 Remember Your word to Your servant, in which You have made me hope.
50 This is my comfort in my affliction, that Your promise gives me life.
51 Godless men utterly derided me, but I do not turn away from Your law.
52 When I think of Your ordinances from of old, I take comfort, O Lord.
53 Hot indignation seizes me because of the wicked, who forsake Your law.
54 Your statutes have been my songs in the house of my exile.
55 I remember Your Name in the night, O Lord, and keep Your law.
56 This blessing has fallen to me because I have kept Your precepts.
57 You are my portion, O Lord; I promise to keep Your words.
58 I entreat Your favor with all my heart; be merciful to me according to Your promise.
59 I thought of Your ways and turned my feet to Your testimonies.
60 I hasten and do not delay to keep Your commandments.
61 Though the cords of the wicked ensnare me, I do not forget Your law.

62 At midnight I rise to praise You, because of Your righteous ordinances.
63 I am a friend of all who fear You and keep Your commandments.
64 The earth, O Lord, is full of Your mercy; teach me Your statutes.
65 You have dealt well with Your servant, O Lord, according to Your word.
66 Teach me good judgment and knowledge, for I believe in Your commandments.
67 Before I was humbled I went astray, but now I keep Your word.
68 You are good, O Lord; in Your goodness teach me Your statutes.
69 The lies of the proud are multiplied against me, but with my whole heart I keep Your precepts.
70 Their heart is soured like milk, but I delight in Your law.
71 It was good for me that You have humbled me, that I might learn Your statutes.
72 The law of Your mouth is better to me than thousands of gold and silver pieces.
73 Your hands have made and fashioned me; give me understanding that I may learn Your commandments.
74 Those who fear You shall see me and rejoice, because I have hoped in Your word.
75 I know, O Lord, that Your judgments are right, and that in Your truth You have afflicted me.
76 Let Your mercy be ready to comfort me, according to Your promise to Your servant.

77 Let Your mercy come to me that I may live, for Your law is my delight.
78 Let the godless be put to shame, because they have transgressed against me unjustly; as for me, I will meditate on Your precepts.
79 Let those who fear You turn to me, that they may know Your testimonies.
80 May my heart be blameless in Your statutes, that I may not be put to shame.
81 My soul languishes for Your salvation; I hope in Your word.
82 My eyes fail with watching for Your promise; I ask, when will You comfort me?
83 For I have become like a wineskin in the smoke, yet I have not forgotten Your statutes.
84 How long must Your servant endure? When will You judge those who persecute me?
85 Godless men have dug pitfalls for me, men who do not conform to Your law.
86 All Your commandments are sure; they persecute me with falsehood; help me!
87 They have almost made an end of me on earth, but I have not forsaken Your precepts.
88 In Your mercy spare my life, that I may keep the commandments of Your mouth.
89 Forever, O Lord, Your word is firmly fixed in the heavens; Your truth endures to all generations.
90 You have established the earth, and it stands fast.
91 The day continues by Your ordinance, for all things are Your servants.
92 If Your law had not been my delight, I should have perished in my affliction.

I will never forget Your precepts; for by them You have given me life.	93
I am Yours; save me, for I have sought Your precepts.	94
The wicked lie in wait to destroy me, but I consider Your testimonies.	95
I have seen that all things come to an end, and Your commandment alone is eternal.	96
Oh, how I love Your law, O Lord! It is my meditation all day long!	97
Your commandment makes me wiser than my enemies, for it is mine forever.	98
I have more understanding than all my teachers, for Your testimonies are my meditation.	99
I understand more than my elders, for I seek Your commandments.	100
I hold back my feet from every evil way in order to keep Your word.	101
I do not turn aside from Your ordinances, for You have taught me.	102
How sweet are Your words to my taste, sweeter than honey to my mouth!	103
Through Your precepts I gain understanding; therefore I hate every false way.	104
Your word is a lamp to my feet and a light to my path.	105
I have sworn an oath and confirmed it, to observe Your righteous ordinances.	106
I am sorely afflicted; give me life, O Lord, according to Your word!	107
Accept my offerings of praise, O Lord, and teach me Your ordinances.	108

109 My soul is continually in my hands, and I have not forgotten Your law.
110 The wicked have laid a snare for me, but I do not stray from Your precepts.
111 Your testimonies are my heritage forever; yes, they are the joy of my heart.
112 I incline my heart to perform Your statutes forever, to the end.
113 I have hated transgressors, but Your law I have loved.
114 You are my hiding place and my defender; I hope in Your word.
115 Depart from me, you evildoers, and I will keep the commandments of my God.
116 Uphold me according to Your promise, that I may live, and let me not be put to shame in my hope.
117 Help me, and I shall be saved, and I will meditate on Your statutes continually.
118 You spurn all who go astray from Your statutes; yes, their cunning is in vain.
119 I have regarded all the wicked of the earth as transgressors; therefore I love Your testimonies.
120 Nail my flesh with the fear of You, for I am afraid of Your judgments.
121 I have done what is just and right; do not leave me to my oppressors.
122 Uphold the welfare of Your servant; let not the godless oppress me.
123 My eyes fail with watching for Your salvation and for the fulfillment of Your righteous promise.
124 Deal with Your servant according to Your mercy, and teach me Your statutes.

I am Your servant; give me understanding, that I may know Your testimonies.	125
It is time for the Lord to act, for they have broken Your law.	126
Therefore I love Your commandments above gold, above fine gold.	127
Therefore, I direct my steps by all Your precepts; I hate every false way.	128
Your testimonies are wonderful; therefore my soul seeks them.	129
The unfolding of Your words gives light; it imparts understanding to the simple.	130
With open mouth I pant, because I long for Your commandments.	131
Look upon me and have mercy on me, as is Your good pleasure toward those who love Your name.	132
Order my steps in Your word, and so shall no wickedness have dominion over me.	133
Deliver me from the wrongful dealings of men, and so shall I keep Your commandments.	134
Shine the light of Your countenance upon Your servant and teach me Your statutes.	135
My eyes shed streams of tears, because men do not keep Your law.	136
Righteous are You, O Lord, and right are Your judgments.	137
You have appointed Your testimonies in righteousness and in all truth.	138
My zeal consumes me, because my foes forget Your words.	139

140 Your promise is well tried in the fire, and Your servant loves it.
141 I am small and despised, yet I do not forget Your precepts.
142 Your righteousness is righteous forever, and Your word is truth.
143 Trouble and anguish have come upon me, but Your commandments are my delight.
144 Your testimonies are righteous forever; give me understanding that I may live.
145 I cry with my whole heart; hear me, O Lord! I will keep Your statutes.
146 I cry to You; save me, that I may observe Your testimonies.
147 I rise before dawn and cry for help; I hope in Your words.
148 My eyes are awake before the morning that I may meditate upon Your promise.
149 Hear my voice according to Your lovingkindness, O Lord; in Your judgment give me life.
150 They draw near who persecute me with evil purpose; they are far from Your law.
151 But You are near, O Lord, and all Your commandments are true.
152 Long have I known from Your testimonies that You have founded them forever.
153 Look on my humiliation and deliver me, for I do not forget Your law.
154 Judge my cause and deliver me; give me life according to Your promise.
155 Salvation is far from the wicked, for they do not seek Your statutes.

Great are Your tender mercies, O Lord; give me life according to Your justice.	156
Many are my persecutors and my adversaries, but I do not swerve from Your testimonies.	157
I look at the faithless with disgust, because they do not keep Your commandments.	158
Consider how I love Your precepts! Give me life according to Your mercy.	159
The sum of Your word is truth, and every one of Your righteous ordinances endures forever.	160
Princes persecute me without cause, but my heart stands in awe of Your words.	161
I rejoice at Your word like one who finds great spoil.	162
I hate and abhor falsehood, but I love Your law.	163
Seven times a day I praise You for Your righteous ordinances.	164
Great peace have those who love Your law; nothing can make them stumble.	165
I hope for Your salvation, O Lord, and I love Your commandments.	166
My soul keeps Your testimonies; I love them exceedingly.	167
I keep Your precepts and testimonies, for all my ways are before You, O Lord.	168
Let my cry come before You, O Lord; give me understanding according to Your word!	169
Let my supplication come before You; deliver me according to Your word.	170
My lips will pour forth praise, for You have taught me Your statutes.	171

172 My tongue will sing of Your word, for all Your commandments are right.
173 Let Your hand be near to save me, for I have chosen Your precepts.
174 I long for Your salvation, O Lord, and Your law is my delight.
175 Let my soul live, that I may praise You, and let Your ordinances help me.
176 I have gone astray like a lost sheep; seek Your servant, for I have not forgotten Your commandments.

✤ ✤ ✤

UNSOCIAL MEDIA

Turn my eyes from looking at vanities, and give me life in Your ways.
PSALM 118:36

Every so often I like to sit down and examine my life and the things I allow to take up space in it. I always discover activities that don't really need to be there, for the simple fact that they don't contribute to anything needful. Social media is always at the top of the list and constantly requires recalibrating. It takes time and effort that I don't always feel like giving, and many times it steals my attention from things that are much more important. Sure, there are people I truly enjoy interacting with, catching glimpses of their lives, and there are others by whom I find myself totally inspired. But it takes constant effort not to fall down the rabbit hole.

One thing I know for sure is that in order for my social media time to be more productive and less distracting, I have to set clear boundaries and be purposeful in my use of it.

Here are a few simple ways to become more intentional online:

» *Remember that facts do not equal wisdom.* Just because you're reading it online doesn't make it so. Choose people and sites that are trustworthy and align with your own personal beliefs.
» *Establish rules.* How many days a week will you check your accounts? For how long? I used to keep my phone on my nightstand to charge at night, and as soon as my alarm went off, I'd reach for it, shut off the alarm, and then scroll through my notifications. It was information overload and not the way I wanted to begin my day. Now, I charge my phone in the kitchen and have turned off most notifications. I also

made a rule not to check social media until I've done morning prayers and read at least one chapter of the Bible or another spiritual book.

» *Follow wisely and unfollow accordingly.* Be careful whom you follow and be aware of how their posts make you feel. If someone posts things you're trying to leave behind, it's probably best not to follow that person. Does an account give you anxiety or incite you? Unfollow. Does a certain brand make you spend money you don't want to spend? Unfollow. Tired of endless selfies and #humblebrags? Unfollow. The only accounts you should let take up space in your feed are the ones that have something positive to offer. Anything less needs to go.

» *Take a break.* Sometimes you just need to unplug. Start small and stay offline for a weekend. Or a week. How about a forty-day fast, or a month during the summer so you can focus on your family instead of your phone? You decide when the best time is, but decide and then do it. I try to stay off during vacations and family activities so I can live those moments fully. Social media will be there to #latergram, I promise.

» *Remember that #reallife isn't real life.* Just because someone's life looks perfect doesn't mean it is. No one's social media life is their real life all the time. In between those curated little squares are tears, struggles, and worries no one else can see. When I post a photo of my freshly brewed coffee next to my Bible on the deck with leaves of every color in the background, it might appear perfect. But what people don't see is my sink full of dishes or that bushel of laundry waiting to be folded or my kids fighting inside, which may be the reason I fled outside to begin with! And while that moment on the deck is real, it's only a tiny glimpse into the big picture of my life. This is the case with every single person on social media. We share the good, while the bad and the ugly remain undocumented.

» *Be stingy with your memories.* Sure, everyone likes to share certain milestones or particularly cute moments, but you know what? Some of them should be held close just for you. Because I have an online presence, I'm expected to post often, and for the most part I do. But there are a lot of moments I'm just too stingy to share, such as when my husband turns on our favorite song and we dance around our room in the dark. Or when one of my children shares a particularly special part of his heart with me. Those precious moments are mine, and if I post them and put them on display for everyone to see, they won't be just mine anymore. I'm simply not willing to give them up.

» *Accept that your life does not need validation from third parties.* You don't need hundreds of likes or comments to confirm that your life is good. No one else needs to see that special moment for it to be real.

Life is so much fuller when we set limitations on the virtual world. There's more time to read or knit or take a walk or snuggle with our littles without distraction. Decide which life is really worth investing in—your spiritual life or your virtual one—and then fill it with the things that truly make your heart happy. If we struggle to fill our lives with good and spiritual things and constantly have prayer on our lips, there will be no room left for the unholy.

*Don't sit, glued to the television. . . .
Guard yourselves from the means of mass blinding.*
ELDER EPIPHANIOS OF ATHENS[1]

---

1 *Precious Vessels of the Holy Spirit*, p. 76.

JOURNALING PAGES

KATHISMA 18

PSALM 119

In my distress I cried to the Lord, and He answered me: 1
"Deliver me, O Lord, from unjust lips and from a deceitful tongue." 2
What shall be given to you? And what more shall be done to you, you deceitful tongue? 3
Sharpened weapons of the Almighty; devastating glowing coals! 4
Woe is me, that my sojourning is prolonged, that 5
I dwell among the tents of Kedar; my soul has long been in exile. 6
I was peaceful among those who hated peace; when I spoke to them, they fought against me without a cause. 7

PSALM 120

I lift up my eyes to the hills, from where my help will come. 1
My help comes from the Lord, who made heaven and earth. 2
He will not let your foot be moved; He who keeps you will not slumber. 3
Behold, He who keeps Israel will neither slumber nor sleep. 4

5 The Lord will keep you; the Lord will be your
   protection at your right hand.
6 The sun shall not smite you by day, nor the moon
   by night.
7 May the Lord keep you from all evil; the Lord
   will keep your soul.
8 The Lord will keep your going out and
   your coming in from this time forth and
   forevermore.

PSALM 121

1 I rejoiced when they said to me, "Let us go to the
   house of the Lord!"
2 Our feet were standing within your gates,
   O Jerusalem!
3 Jerusalem is built as a city whose features are
   harmoniously composed.
4 For there the tribes went up, the tribes of the
   Lord, as a decree for Israel, to give thanks to
   the name of the Lord.
5 There thrones for judgment are set, the thrones of
   the house of David.
6 Pray now for the peace of Jerusalem and for
   prosperity for those who love you!
7 Let peace be in your strongholds and prosperity
   within your palaces!
8 For my brethren and neighbors' sake, I have
   spoken peace concerning you.
9 For the sake of the house of the Lord our God, I
   have diligently sought your good.

PSALM 122

To You I lift up my eyes, who are enthroned in the heavens! 1
Behold, as the eyes of servants look to the hand of their master, 2
as the eyes of a maid to the hand of her mistress,
so our eyes look to the Lord our God, till He have mercy on us.
Have mercy on us, O Lord, have mercy on us, for we have had more than enough of contempt. 3
Too long our soul has been sated with the scorn of those who are at ease, the contempt of the proud. 4

PSALM 123

If it had not been that the Lord was among us, let Israel now say, 1
if it had not been that the Lord was among us, when men rose up against us, 2
they would indeed have swallowed us up alive when their anger was kindled against us; 3
indeed, the flood would have swept us away; our soul would have gone under the torrent; 4
indeed our soul would have gone under the raging waters. 5
Blessed be the Lord, who has not given us as prey to their teeth! 6

7 Our soul has been delivered like a bird from the snare of the fowler; the snare is broken, and we are delivered!

8 Our help is in the name of the Lord, who made heaven and earth!

PSALM 124

1 Those who trust in the Lord are like Mount Zion. He that dwells in Jerusalem will never be shaken.

2 As the mountains are round about Jerusalem, so the Lord is round about His people, from this time forth and forevermore.

3 For the Lord will not allow the scepter of sinners to rest upon the lot of the righteous, lest the righteous put forth their hands to do wrong.

4 Do good, O Lord, to those who are good and to those who are upright in heart!

5 But those who turn aside upon their crooked ways the Lord will lead away with evildoers.
Peace be in Israel!

PSALM 125

1 When the Lord brought back the captives of Zion, we became like those who are comforted.

2 Then our mouth was filled with joy and our tongue with exultation;
then they said among the nations, "The Lord has done great things for them."

The Lord had done great things for us; we were filled with joy. 3
O Lord, bring back our captives like the streams in the south; those who sow in tears will reap in joy! 4 5
They went forth weeping as they sowed their seeds; but they will surely come with exultation, bringing their sheaves with them. 6

PSALM 126

Unless the Lord builds the house, those who build it labor in vain. 1
Unless the Lord watches over the city, the watchman stays awake in vain.
It is in vain that you rise up early, rising up from rest, eating the bread of anxious toil; for He gives to His beloved sleep. 2
Lo, children are a heritage from the Lord, the fruit of the womb a reward. 3
Like arrows in the hand of a mighty man are the sons of one's youth. 4
Blessed is the man who has his quiver full of them! 5
He will not be put to shame when he speaks with his enemies in the gate.

PSALM 127

Blessed are all those who fear the Lord, those who walk in His ways! 1

2 You shall eat of the fruit of your labor; you shall be blessed and filled with good things.
3 Your wife shall be like a fruitful vine within your house;
your children will be like olive shoots around your table.
4 Lo, thus shall the man be blessed who fears the Lord.
5 May the Lord bless you from Zion, and may you see the good things of Jerusalem all the days of your life!
6 And may you see your children's children! Peace be upon Israel!

PSALM 128

1 "Often have they fought me from my youth," let Israel now say.
2 "Often have they fought me from my youth," yet they have not prevailed against me.
3 The sinners worked upon my back; they lengthened their wickedness.
4 The Lord is righteous; He has broken the necks of the wicked.
5 May all who hate Zion be put to shame and turned backward!
6 Let them be like the grass on the housetops, which withers before it grows up,
7 with which the reaper does not fill his hand or the binder of sheaves his bosom.

And those who pass by do not say, "The blessing of the Lord be upon you! We bless you in the name of the Lord!" 8

PSALM 129

Out of the depths I cry to You, O Lord. Lord, hear my voice. 1

Let Your ears be attentive to the voice of my supplication. 2

If You, O Lord, should mark iniquities, Lord, who could stand? 3

But there is forgiveness with You, that You may be feared. 4

For Your name's sake I have waited for You, O Lord; my soul has hoped on the Lord. 5

From the morning watch until night, from the morning watch, let Israel hope on the Lord. 6

For with the Lord there is steadfast love, and with Him is plenteous redemption, 7

and He will deliver Israel from all his iniquities. 8

PSALM 130

O Lord, my heart is not lifted up; my eyes are not raised too high; 1

I did not delve into things too great and too marvelous for me.

If I have not kept my heart humble, but have lifted up my soul; 2

if I have not remained like a weaned child
by his mother's side, let my soul receive its recompense.
3 Let Israel hope in the Lord from this time forth and forevermore.

PSALM 131

1 O Lord, remember David and all his meekness;
2 how he swore to the Lord and vowed to the God of Jacob:
3 "I will not enter the tent of my house; I will not go up to the couch of my bed;
4 I will not give sleep to my eyes or slumber to my eyelids or rest to my temples,
5 until I find a place for the Lord, a dwelling place for the God of Jacob."
6 Lo, we heard of it in Ephratha; we found it in the fields of the wood.
7 "Let us enter His dwelling place; let us worship at the place where His feet stood!"
8 Arise, O Lord, into Your resting place, You and the ark of Your holiness!
9 Your priests will be clothed in righteousness, and Your saints shall rejoice.
10 For Your servant David's sake, do not turn away the face of Your Anointed.
11 The Lord swore in truth to David, from which He will not turn back:
"Of the fruit of your body, I will set upon your throne.

If your sons will keep My covenant and My testimonies which I shall teach them, their sons also forever shall sit upon your throne." 12

For the Lord has chosen Zion; He has desired it for His habitation: 13

"This is my resting place forever; here I will dwell, for I have desired it. 14

I will abundantly bless her provisions; I will satisfy her poor with bread. 15

Her priests I will clothe with salvation, and her saints will shout for joy. 16

There I will make a horn to sprout for David; I have prepared a lamp for my Anointed. 17

His enemies I will clothe with shame, but upon Him my sanctification will flourish." 18

PSALM 132

Behold, how good and pleasant it is when brothers dwell in unity. 1

It is like myrrh upon the head that runs down the beard, the beard of Aaron, that runs down the collar of his robe. 2

It is like the dew of Hermon which falls on the mountains of Zion. 3

For there the Lord commanded the blessing: life forevermore.

PSALM 133

1 Behold, now bless the Lord, all you servants of the Lord,
 you that stand in the house of the Lord, in the courts of the house of our God.
2 Lift up your hands by night to the Holy of Holies and bless the Lord!
3 May the Lord bless you from Zion, He who made heaven and earth!

✠ ✠ ✠

RAISING ARROWS

Like arrows in the hand of a mighty man are the sons of one's youth.

PSALM 126:3

Our job as parents today is harder than ever. Society has trained us to rely too much on others to raise the precious children God has entrusted to us. We willingly hand them over to various teachers, coaches, and advisors, so they're oftentimes learning from people whose main goal may not be salvation.

I remember speaking to a holy elder around the time my oldest was getting ready to start school. We were having a conversation about homeschooling versus public school. After discussing the pros and cons of each, he said something I've kept in the back of my mind ever since: "As Christian parents we must be ready to deprogram and reprogram our children each and every time they return from the world." In other words, we need to spend time each and every day talking to our children about their day. Not only about the things they learned in the classroom, but what kind of conversations took place during lunch or at the bus stop. Did anything happen that made them feel happy or sad or uncomfortable? Then talk about Christlike ways to respond to those various situations.

I've always had a homeschooling-mama heart, so when my husband and I made the decision to send our children to public school, I immediately went into watchdog mode, making sure to stay even more vigilant over my precious children. At the beginning of each year, I made sure their teachers were made aware of our beliefs, such as how our kids fasted on Wednesdays and Fridays and didn't participate in certain holidays. I politely asked them to notify me prior to any questionable lessons and made sure I was physically present at the school by volunteering regularly.

The first few times I had to have these conversations, I was a little nervous, worrying that my concerns wouldn't be taken seriously. But through the grace of God, every teacher we had respected our decisions. Some even went out of their way to find alternate assignments when necessary or skipped questionable ones altogether. We even had a teacher ask to come to church with us. On the rare occasion an issue did arise, we took the opportunity to teach our children about the defenders of our Faith and how, in a smaller way, we were being called to do the same.

Despite how wonderful our public school experience was, I always felt deep down that it was just a matter of time before the scales tipped out of its favor. My husband and I made the decision that no matter how great an education our children might be receiving on an academic level, if the atmosphere became spiritually harmful, we would withdraw them.

And sure enough, two years ago we found ourselves at that crossroad with our middle-schooler. Despite the fact that he was in one of the best schools in our area, in no way was his education worth the indoctrination and spiritual ruin he was being faced with in school. Christian beliefs were no longer tolerated in school, but somehow Islamic prayers were making their way home in his backpack. That was just the final straw in a handful of questionable issues that arose that year. I expressed my concerns to the principal, and after careful thought and lots of prayer, we decided he wouldn't return to public school the following year. The year after that, we withdrew our other two children.

Thus began our homeschooling journey. Lord knows our first year was a constant learning experience, as every year will surely be. It was full of trial and error, laughter and tears. Did I mention tears? There were moments when I thought I had ruined my sons' lives forever.

But the more time passes, the more I realize how much more I'm able to give them. Before my very eyes, their characters are transforming.

They've grown and learned in ways I never saw in the eight years we were in the public school system. That fills me with hope and keeps me going. Being able to attend weekday liturgies and study the lives of the saints in greater depth, and having the opportunity all day, every day to teach them Orthodoxy as a way of life has been the biggest blessing. Not to mention the benefits of being able to tailor their studies to their own levels and interests.

I'll certainly never say homeschooling is the answer for every family or even that I regret my children's time in public school, because I don't. I just know that this is what my children need right now, and I'm grateful to be in the position to provide it. In the end, it's not about where your child learns as much as it is what and how he learns. What matters most is that we work hard to take advantage of every opportunity to teach our children how to live as faithful Christians in the world.

We invest everything in our children. We invest in their educations by sending them to the best schools and getting them tutors; we invest in their hobbies by taxiing them to sports and other extracurricular activities; we even invest in their social lives by taking them on play dates and paying for their tickets to go to the movies with friends. But what do we invest in their spiritual lives? Are we teaching them the importance of fasting, praying, communing, and confessing? Do we attend services together? Do we read the lives of the saints?

As parents, our number one priority is to teach our children to live as true Orthodox Christians. Otherwise, the world will teach them not to.

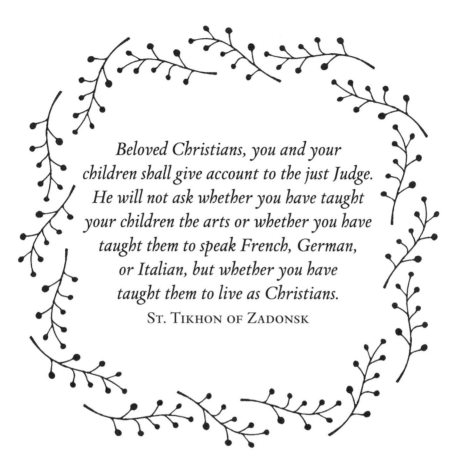

Beloved Christians, you and your children shall give account to the just Judge. He will not ask whether you have taught your children the arts or whether you have taught them to speak French, German, or Italian, but whether you have taught them to live as Christians.
　　St. Tikhon of Zadonsk

JOURNALING PAGES

KATHISMA 19

PSALM 134

P̲raise the name of the Lord; give praise, O servants of the Lord,   1

You that stand in the house of the Lord, in the courts of the house of our God.   2

Praise the Lord, for the Lord is good; sing to His name, for He is gracious,   3

For the Lord has chosen Jacob for Himself, Israel as His own possession.   4

For I know that the Lord is great and that our Lord is above all gods.   5

Whatever the Lord pleases, He does, in heaven and on earth, in the seas and all deeps.   6

He it is who makes the clouds rise at the end of the earth,   7

who makes lightning for the rain and brings forth the wind from His storehouses.

He it was who smote the firstborn of Egypt, both of man and of beast;   8

Who in your midst, O Egypt, sent signs and wonders against Pharaoh and all his servants.   9

Who smote many nations and slew mighty kings—   10

Sihon, King of the Amorites, and Og, King of Bashan,   11

12 and all the kingdoms of Canaan, and gave their land as a heritage, a heritage to His people Israel.
13 Your name, O Lord, endures forever, Your renown, O Lord, throughout all ages.
14 For the Lord will vindicate His people and have compassion on His servants.
15 The idols of the nations are silver and gold, the work of men's hands.
16 They have mouths, but they speak not; they have eyes, but they see not.
17 They have ears, but they hear not, nor is there any breath in their mouths.
18 Let those who make them be like them—yea, everyone who trusts in them.
19 O house of Israel, bless the Lord. O house of Aaron, bless the Lord.
20 O house of Levi, bless the Lord; you that fear the Lord, bless the Lord.
21 Blessed be the Lord from Zion, He who dwells in Jerusalem. Alleluia.

PSALM 135

1 O give thanks to the Lord, for He is good; O give
2 thanks to the God of gods;
3 O give thanks to the Lord of lords, for His steadfast love endures forever.
4 To Him who alone does great wonders, to Him
5 who by understanding made the heavens, for His steadfast love endures forever.

To Him who spread out the earth upon the waters,	6
to Him who made the great lights, for His steadfast love endures forever.	7
The sun to rule over the day, the moon and stars to rule over the night, for His steadfast love endures forever.	8 9
To Him who smote the firstborn of Egypt and brought Israel out from among them,	10 11
with a strong hand and an outstretched arm, for His steadfast love endures forever.	12
To Him who divided the Red Sea asunder and made Israel pass through the midst of it,	13 14
But overthrew Pharaoh and his host in the Red Sea, for His steadfast love endures forever.	15
To Him who led His people through the wilderness, to Him who smote great kings	16 17
And slew famous kings, for His steadfast love endures forever.	18
Sihon, King of the Amorites, and Og, King of Bashan, for His steadfast love endures forever.	19 20
And gave their land as a heritage, a heritage to Israel His servant, for His steadfast love endures forever.	21 22
It is He who remembered us in our low estate and rescued us from our foes,	23 24
He who gives food to all flesh, for His steadfast love endures forever.	25
O give thanks to the God of heaven, for His steadfast love endures forever. Alleluia.	26

✠ ✠ ✠

PSALM 136

1 By the waters of Babylon, there we sat down and wept when we remembered Zion.
2 On the willows there we hung up our lyres.
3 For there our captors required of us sacred songs, and those who led us away, hymns, saying, "Sing us one of the songs of Zion."
4 How shall we sing the Lord's song in a foreign land?
5 If I forget you, O Jerusalem, let my right hand be forgotten!
6 Let my tongue cleave to my throat if I do not remember you, if I do not set Jerusalem above my highest joy!
7 Remember, O Lord, the sons of Edom in the day of Jerusalem, who said, "Raze it, raze it, down to its foundations!"
8 O wretched daughter of Babylon, blessed shall he be who repays you with what you have done to us!
9 Blessed shall he be who takes your little ones and dashes them against the rock!

PSALM 137

1 I will give You thanks, O Lord, with my whole heart; before the angels I will sing psalms to You,
for You have heard all the words of my mouth;

I will worship toward Your holy temple and confess   2
    Your name for Your mercy and Your truth;
for You have exalted above everything Your holy
    name.
On the day I call upon You, hear me; in Your   3
    strength, You will multiply Your care for my
    soul.
Let all the kings of the earth confess You,   4
    O Lord, for they have heard all the words
    of Your mouth;
and let them sing of the ways of the Lord, for   5
    great is the glory of the Lord.
For though the Lord is high, He regards the lowly;   6
    but the haughty He knows from afar.
If I walk in the midst of trouble, You will give me   7
    life;
You have stretched out Your hand against the
    wrath of my enemies, and Your right hand
    delivered me.
O Lord, you will fulfill Your purpose for me;   8
Your mercy, O Lord, endures forever. Do not
    despise the works of Your hands.

PSALM 138

O Lord, You have tested me and known me!   1
You know when I lie down and when I awake; You   2
    discern my thoughts from afar.
You have known my path and the extent of my   3
    life, and have foreseen all my ways, that there is   4
    no unrighteous word on my tongue.

5 Lo, O Lord, You know all things: the last and the first.
You have fashioned me and laid Your hand upon me.
6 Your knowledge is too wonderful for me; it is high, I cannot attain it.
7 Where shall I go from Your Spirit? And where shall I flee from Your Face?
8 If I ascend to heaven, You are there! If I go down to Sheol, You are there!
9 If I take my wings toward the morning and dwell in the uttermost parts of the sea,
10 even there Your hand shall lead me, and Your right hand shall hold me.
11 And I said, "Surely the darkness will cover me," but even the night itself became light in my joy.
12 For darkness will not be dark to You, but the night will be bright as the day; darkness will be as light.
13 For You, O Lord, formed my inward parts; You knitted me together in my mother's womb.
14 I will give thanks to You, for I am fearfully and wondrously made.
Marvelous are Your works, and my soul knows it in a manner beyond understanding!
15 My bones which You made in secret were not hidden from You, nor my substance in the depths of the earth.
16 Your eyes beheld my unformed substance,
and in Your book they all were written, the days that You were yet to make, and none of them were missing.

Your friends are greatly honored in my eyes, O God; their rule is very great!	17
I will count them, and they will be multiplied more than the sand.	18
When I awake, I am still with You.	
O that You would slay the wicked, O God!	19
Depart from me, O men of blood, for you are quarrelsome in your thoughts.	
It is in vain that they will take Your cities, O Lord.	20
Have I not hated those who hate You? And have I not wasted away from zeal because of Your enemies?	21
I hated them with perfect hatred; they became my enemies.	22
Test me, O God, and know my heart! Try me and know my paths!	23
And see if there be any wicked way in me, and lead me in the way everlasting!	24

PSALM 139

Deliver me, O Lord, from evil men; rescue me from violent men	1
who plot iniquity in their heart and stir up wars all the day.	2
They have made their tongue sharp as a serpent's, and under their lips is the poison of vipers.	3
Guard me, O Lord, from the hand of the sinner; deliver me from violent men who have planned to overthrow my steps.	4

5 Arrogant men have hidden a trap for me, and with cords they have spread a net; by the wayside they have set a stumbling block for me.
6 I say to the Lord, "You are my God; give ear to the voice of my supplications, O Lord!"
7 Lord, O Lord, the strength of my salvation, You will cover my head in the day of battle.
8 According to my desires, O Lord, do not hand me over to the wicked.
They have taken counsel against me; do not forsake me, lest they be exalted.
9 On the heads of those who surround me will fall the mischief of their lips!
10 Burning coals will fall upon them; You will cast them down into the fire, into unbearable afflictions.
11 A gossip will not prosper in the land; evils will hunt down the unrighteous man to destruction.
12 I know that the Lord will maintain the cause of the poor and the right of the needy.
13 Surely the righteous will give thanks to Your name; the upright will dwell before Your Face.

PSALM 140

1 Lord, I call upon You; hear me. Hear me, O Lord. Lord, I call upon You; hear me. Receive the voice of my prayer when I call upon You.
2 Let my prayer arise in Your sight as incense, and let the lifting up of my hands be an evening sacrifice. Hear me, O Lord.

Set a guard over my mouth, O Lord; keep watch over the door of my lips! 3

Incline not my heart to any evil, to busy myself with wicked deeds in company with men who work iniquity; and let me not partake of their delights! 4

Let a good man strike or rebuke me in kindness, but let the oil of the wicked never anoint my head, for my prayer is continually against their wicked deeds. 5

When they are given over to those who shall condemn them, then they shall learn that the word of the Lord is true. 6

As a rock which one cleaves and shatters on the land, so shall their bones be strewn at the mouth of Sheol. 7

But my eyes are toward You, O Lord God; in You I seek refuge; leave me not defenseless! 8

Keep me from the trap which they have laid for me and from the snares of evildoers! 9

Let the wicked together fall into their own nets, while I escape. 10

PSALM 141

I cry with my voice to the Lord; with my voice I make supplication to the Lord. 1

I pour out my complaint before Him; I tell my trouble before Him. 2

When my spirit is faint, You know my way. 3

In the path where I walk they have hidden a trap
  for me.
4 I look to the right and watch, but there is none
  who takes notice of me;
no refuge remains to me, no man cares for me.
5 I cry to You, O Lord; I say, "You are my refuge,
  my portion in the land of the living."
6 Give heed to my cry, for I am brought very low!
Deliver me from my persecutors, for they are too
  strong for me.
7 Bring my soul out of prison, that I may give
  thanks to Your name!
The righteous will surround me, for You will deal
  bountifully with me.

PSALM 142

1 Hear my prayer, O Lord; give ear to my
  supplications! In Your faithfulness answer me,
  in Your righteousness!
2 Enter not into judgment with Your servant; for no
  man living is righteous before You.
3 For the enemy has pursued me; he has crushed
  my life to the ground; he has made me sit in
  darkness like those long dead.
4 Therefore my spirit faints within me; my heart
  within me is appalled.
5 I remember the days of old; I meditate on all that
  You have done; I muse on what Your hands have
  wrought.

I stretch out my hands to You; my soul thirsts for 6
    You like a parched land.

Make haste to answer me, O Lord! My spirit fails! 7
Hide not Your Face from me, lest I be like those
    who go down to the Pit.

Let me hear in the morning of Your steadfast love, 8
    for in You I put my trust.

Teach me the way I should go, for to You I lift up
    my soul.

Deliver me, O Lord, from my enemies! I have fled 9
    to You for refuge!

Teach me to do Your will, for You are my God. 10
Let Your good Spirit lead me on a level path.

For Your name's sake, O Lord, preserve my life. 11
In Your righteousness bring me out of trouble.

And in Your steadfast love cut off my enemies 12
    and destroy all my adversaries, for I am Your
    servant.

✠ ✠ ✠

THROUGH THE INTERCESSIONS

Your friends are greatly honored in my eyes, O God.
PSALM 138:17

People who are unfamiliar with Orthodoxy often ask why we waste our time praying to the saints instead of praying directly to God. I always respond that we ask for the intercessions of the saints for the same reason people went to the apostles for healing, even when Christ was still on earth with them. Why didn't those people go straight to Jesus? Or why do we ask our friends to pray for us? Isn't it the same thing? Christ said that if we believe in Him we never die, so does it really matter if the saints have fallen asleep to this life?

Orthodoxy is a Kingdom, Christ's Kingdom on earth. We read in the Bible of all the miracles God worked through the apostles. We read in Acts about the miracles God worked through the prayers of St. Paul, even through his aprons and handkerchiefs, or how people were healed by the shadow of St. Peter. Why would that change? Doesn't it say in the Bible that Jesus Christ is the same yesterday, today, and forever (Heb. 13:8)? Or should we simply choose scripture verses that accommodate our prejudices?

We know that without the power of God, even our greatest wonder-working saints would be powerless, because every good and perfect gift is from above. It is only by the grace and mercy of God that miracles are worked through them, but they are worked through them. And through them we give all the glory to God. Every hymn we chant or prayer we utter to them in turn glorifies God.

For example, this hymn to St. Nektarios:

The offspring of Selyvria and guardian of Aegina,
A true friend of virtue who appeared in the latter years,
O Nektarios, we faithful honor you as a godly servant of Christ.
For you pour forth healing of every kind on those who piously cry out:
Glory to Christ who has glorified you,
Glory to Him who has made you wondrous,
Glory to Him who works healings for all through you.

The lives of the saints are living examples of how to live a life dedicated to God in a fallen and sinful world. They teach us how to overcome our passions and grow spiritually. The saints are arrows in our spiritual quiver. Everything about their lives points the way to Him. Let us never doubt or underestimate the power of their speedy intercessions.

What does the daily invocation of the saints signify? It signifies that God's saints live, and are near us, ever ready to help us, by the grace of God. We live together with them in the house of our Heavenly Father, only in different parts of it. We can converse with them, and they with us. God's saints are near to the believing heart, and are ready in a moment to help those who call upon them with faith and love.

St. John of Kronstadt[1]

---

[1] I. I. Sergiev and Nicholas Kotar, trans., *My Life in Christ: The Spiritual Journals of St John of Kronstadt* (Jordanville, NY: Holy Trinity Publications, 2015).

JOURNALING PAGES

PSALM 143

Blessed be the Lord my God, who trains my hands for war and my fingers for battle; 1
my mercy and my refuge, my helper and my deliverer, 2
my protector in whom I have trusted, who subdues the peoples under me.
O Lord, what is man that You make Yourself known to him, or the son of man that You take him into account? 3
Man is like vanity; his days are like a passing shadow. 4
Bow Your heavens, O Lord, and come down! Touch the mountains, and they shall smoke! 5
Flash forth the lightning and scatter them; send out Your arrows and rout them! 6
Stretch forth Your hand from on high; rescue me and deliver me from the many waters, 7
from the hands of the sons of strangers, whose mouths speak vanity and whose right hand is a right hand of unrighteousness. 8
I will sing a new song to You, O God; upon a ten-stringed harp I will play to You, 9
to You who give victory to kings, who rescued David Your servant from the cruel sword. 10

11 Deliver me and rescue me from the hands of the sons of strangers, whose mouths speak vanity and whose right hand is a right hand of unrighteousness.
12 Their sons are strengthened in their youth like plants; their daughters are made beautiful, richly adorned like the structure of a palace.
13 Their garners are full, overflowing with all manner of store;
their sheep are prolific, multiplying in their folds; their oxen are fat.
14 There is no breach or fissure in their walls, nor any outcry in their squares.
15 They have called people who are like this blessed, but blessed are the people whose God is the Lord!

PSALM 144

1 I will extol You, my God and King, and bless Your name forever and ever.
2 Every day I will bless You and praise Your name forever and ever.
3 Great is the Lord, and greatly to be praised, and His greatness is unsearchable.
4 One generation shall laud Your works to another and shall declare Your mighty acts.
5 They shall speak of the glorious splendor of Your holiness and recount Your wondrous works.
6 Men shall proclaim the might of Your terrible acts and declare Your greatness.

7   They shall pour forth the fame of Your abundant goodness and shall sing aloud of Your righteousness.
8   The Lord is compassionate and merciful, long-suffering and abounding in mercy.
9   The Lord is good to all, and His compassions are over all that He has made.
10 Let all Your works give thanks to You, O Lord, and let Your saints bless You!
11 They shall speak of the glory of Your kingdom and tell of Your power,
12 to make known to the sons of men Your power and the glorious splendor of Your kingdom.
13 Your kingdom is an everlasting kingdom, and Your dominion endures throughout all generations. The Lord is true in all His words and holy in all His works.
14 The Lord upholds all who are falling and raises up all who are bowed down.
15 The eyes of all look to You, and You give them their food in due season.
16 You open Your hand; You fill every living thing with blessing.
17 The Lord is righteous in all His ways and holy in all His works.
18 The Lord is near to all who call upon Him, to all who call upon Him in truth.
19 He will fulfill the desire of those who fear Him, and He will hear their cry and save them.
20 The Lord preserves all who love Him, but all the wicked He will destroy.

21 My mouth will speak the praise of the Lord, and let all flesh bless His holy name forever and ever.

PSALM 145

1 Praise the Lord! Praise the Lord, O my soul!
2 I will praise the Lord as long as I live; I will sing praises to my God while I have being.
3 Put not your trust in princes, in sons of men, in whom there is no salvation.
4 When his breath departs, he returns to his earth; on that very day his plans perish.
5 Blessed is he whose help is the God of Jacob, whose hope is in the Lord his God,
6 who made heaven and earth, the sea, and all that is in them;
7 who keeps faith forever; who executes justice for the oppressed; who gives food to the hungry.
8 The Lord sets the prisoners free; the Lord opens the eyes of the blind.
The Lord lifts up those who are bowed down; the Lord loves the righteous.
9 The Lord watches over the sojourners; He upholds the widow and the fatherless; but the way of the wicked He brings to ruin.
10 The Lord will reign forever, Your God, O Zion, to all generations. Praise the Lord!

PSALM 146

1. Praise the Lord, for it is good to sing praises to our God. Let our praises be pleasing to Him!
2. The Lord builds up Jerusalem; He gathers the outcasts of Israel.
3. He heals the brokenhearted and binds up their wounds.
4. He determines the number of the stars; He calls them all by name.
5. Great is our God and abundant in power. His understanding is beyond measure!
6. The Lord lifts up the meek but casts the sinners to the ground.
7. Intone a song of thanksgiving to the Lord; sing praises upon the harp to our God!
8. Who covers the heavens with clouds, who prepares rain for the earth, Who makes grass grow upon the hills and herbs for the use of men,
9. and gives to the beasts their food, and to the young ravens which cry to Him.
10. His delight will not be in the strength of the horse nor His pleasure in the legs of a man;
11. but the Lord takes pleasure in those who fear Him, in those who hope in His mercy.

✣ ✣ ✣

PSALM 147

1. Praise the Lord, O Jerusalem! Praise your God, O Zion!
2. For He strengthens the bars of your gates; He blesses your sons within you.
3. He makes peace in your borders; He fills you with the finest of the wheat.
4. He sends forth His word to the earth; His proclamation runs swiftly.
5. He gives snow like wool; He scatters the mist like ashes.
6. He casts forth His ice like crumbs; who shall stand before His cold?
7. He will send forth His word and melt them; He will blow with His Spirit and the waters will flow.
8. He declares His word to Jacob, His statutes and judgments to Israel.
9. He has not dealt thus with any other nation and has not shown His judgments to them.

PSALM 148

1. Praise the Lord! Praise the Lord from heaven, praise Him in the highest!
2. Praise Him, all you angels of His! Praise Him, all His hosts!
3. Praise Him, sun and moon; praise Him, all you stars and light.

Praise Him, you highest heavens and you waters above the heavens. 4

Let them praise the name of the Lord, for He spoke and they came to be; He commanded, and they were created. 5

He established them forever and ever; He set a law which cannot pass away. 6

Praise the Lord from the earth, you sea monsters and all deeps, 7

fire and hail, snow and frost, stormy winds fulfilling His word. 8

Mountains and all hills, fruit trees and all cedars, 9

beasts and all cattle, creeping things and flying birds, 10

kings of the earth and all peoples, princes and rulers of the earth, 11

young men and maidens together, old men and children: 12

Let them praise the name of the Lord, for His name alone is exalted; He is acknowledged in heaven and on earth; 13

and He will raise up a horn for His people—a song for all His saints, the sons of Israel who are near to Him. Praise the Lord! 14

PSALM 149

Praise the Lord! Sing to the Lord a new song, His praise in the church of the faithful. 1

Let Israel be glad in his Maker; let the sons of Zion rejoice in their King. 2

3 Let them praise His name with dancing, making melody to Him with timbrel and psalms.
4 For the Lord takes pleasure in His people and exalts the humble in salvation.
5 Let the faithful exult in glory; let them sing for joy on their beds.
6 Let the high praises of God be in their throats and two-edged swords in their hands,
7 to wreak vengeance on the nations and chastisement on the peoples;
8 to bind their kings with chains and their nobles with iron fetters,
9 to execute on them the judgment written; this is glory for all His saints.
Praise the Lord!

PSALM 150

1 Praise the Lord! Praise God in His sanctuary; praise Him in His mighty firmament.
2 Praise Him for His powers; praise Him according to His exceeding greatness.
3 Praise Him with trumpet sound; praise Him in psalms and harp.
4 Praise Him with timbrel and dance; praise Him with strings and pipe.
5 Praise Him with sounding cymbals; praise Him with loud clashing cymbals!
6 Let every breath praise the Lord! Praise the Lord!

DO ~~GOOD~~ BETTER

The eyes of all look to You,
and You give them their food in due season.
Psalm 144:15

Few things bring me as much joy as serving others. I love to make others happy and consider it an incredible blessing to play even the smallest role in something that can potentially make a difference in someone else's life. Don't think this entirely selfless, though, as I often take away more from these experiences than I could ever hope to offer. Helping others helps me keep things in perspective by reminding me that there are a lot of people with real needs and that most of my so-called needs are superficial in comparison.

I'll never forget the missions trip to Alaska my husband and I took with the OCMC. We went there with our luggage full of books, coloring sheets, and prayer ropes to give to the Native people we would meet. And we did that. But what they gave us in return was something much more than we could ever have imagined. They showed us true, living Orthodoxy. My eyes were opened to a new and more humble way of life. The joy that shone from the people's faces and voices as they sang hymns so familiar, yet so unfamiliar in their Yupik tongue, took hold of my heart and changed me forever. I'd known happiness in life, but I had never known the kind of joy these beautiful people had.

We returned to the Lower Forty-Eight a month later with a renewed understanding of serving others. I couldn't volunteer at enough shelters and soup kitchens. My soul yearned to be close to the poor, sick, and elderly. Christ loved them, and I had finally gained a small understanding of why. I could feel something words can't quite describe radiating from them. Even the homeless man smelling of liquor possessed some intangible quality that made me want to love him.

I'm constantly on the lookout for situations where God might use me. I try to be open to that idea, being willing to step outside my comfort zone in an effort to do what I think He requires of me. Sometimes it feels like second nature; other times it feels completely awkward. But it always feels right.

My kids love driving around town delivering lunches we've packed to the hungry on the sides of the road. We always ask their names so we can do a round on our prayer ropes for them, and because of this we've come to know many of them quite well. I also volunteer as a wish granter for the Make-A-Wish Foundation and have the blessing of working closely with children with critical illnesses. My time spent with them is a daily reminder of the good in this world.

Christ described them as "the least of these" by worldly standards, but in my eyes they are the greatest of us all. And we are so fortunate to have the opportunity to serve them.

Even in our day and age, there are so many people in need of the most basic of life's necessities. While we may not be able to make a difference for everyone, if we just make a difference for someone, that is enough.

When you have the opportunity to do good, do not let it go by.
ST. POLYKARP OF SMYRNA

JOURNALING PAGES

TOPICAL INDEX
of needs for which various psalms may be read

AGRICULTURE: 1, 26, 30, 50, 52, 62, 66, 71, 83, 124, 147, 148

ANIMALS, Unfriendly: 63, 123, 147

CHILDREN: 22, 76, 109, 113, 114

DEATH AND DEPARTED: 33, 150

DISASTERS: 17, 21, 30, 50, 62, 68, 85, 89

HEALTH, Physical: 5, 12, 28, 36, 37, 44, 56, 58, 63, 79, 86, 88, 95, 102, 108, 122, 125, 128, 145, 146

HEALTH, Psychological: 4, 7, 8, 9, 11, 24, 27, 41, 55, 56, 60, 61, 69, 70, 80, 81, 84, 97, 100, 103, 128, 136, 138

HEALTH, Women's: 18, 19, 40, 67, 75, 106, 142, 145

LAW AND GOVERNMENT: 14, 16, 32, 36, 47, 51, 59, 72, 82, 84, 93, 101, 108, 110, 137, 140, 141, 143

MAGIC AND DEMONS: 5, 6, 8, 9, 13, 33, 57, 65, 90, 94, 96, 121

PEACE AND WAR: 26, 33, 42, 73, 78, 93, 107, 111, 117, 118, 120, 127, 131, 132, 135, 140, 141, 143

PEACE (among friends and family): 10, 19, 22, 35, 41, 43, 45, 54, 65, 76, 86, 94, 109, 116, 126, 127, 139

PROPERTY: 14, 15, 23, 47, 83, 103, 124

PROTECTION: 9, 13, 34, 47, 48, 57, 90, 133

SOCIAL CONCERNS: 20, 32, 35, 38, 51, 53, 59, 77, 80, 81, 87, 93, 101, 110, 112, 113, 114, 119, 124, 137, 140

SPIRITUALITY: 3, 9, 24, 25, 29, 49, 50, 57, 72, 91, 98, 99, 100, 104, 105, 108, 115, 119, 130, 134, 136, 149

TRAVEL AND EMIGRATION: 28, 29, 31, 92, 135, 150

WORK: 2, 38, 39, 46, 48, 51, 52, 57, 60, 64, 74, 81, 83, 100, 101, 103, 129, 137, 140, 144

This index was prepared by the Saint Pachomius Orthodox Library based on the Blessing Psalter of St. Arsenios of Cappadocia. The full list of needs arranged by psalm number is specific to Anatolian village life in the early twentieth century and therefore is more of interest as a historical document than of use to contemporary Americans. It may be found online at http://www.voskrese.info/spl/arsenios.html.

Ancient Faith Publishing hopes you have enjoyed and benefited from this book. The proceeds from the sales of our books only partially cover the costs of operating our nonprofit ministry—which includes both the work of **Ancient Faith Publishing** and the work of **Ancient Faith Radio**. Your financial support makes it possible to continue this ministry both in print and online. Donations are tax-deductible and can be made at **www.ancientfaith.com**.

To view our other publications,
please log onto our website: **store.ancientfaith.com**

Bringing you Orthodox Christian music, readings,
prayers, teaching, and podcasts 24 hours a day since 2004 at
www.ancientfaith.com